trans formed

one congregation's response

to the Second Vatican Council and the Calls of the World

General Editors:
Bonnie Kearney, RSCJ
Diane Roche, RSCJ

Transformed: One Congregation's Response to Vatican II and the World

ISBN 978-1-7364924-2-0

Book design: Beth Ponticello, cedc.org
Photographs: Society of the Sacred Heart Archives

Printed in the United States of America

Published by:
Society of the Sacred Heart
United States – Canada
4120 Forest Park Avenue
St. Louis, Missouri 63108
rscj.org

Table of Contents

Foreword

Women's religious congregations began embracing the teachings of the Second Vatican Council even before the council closed and, in the decades since, have consistently incorporated those teachings into their communal lives and practices.

When *Perfectae Caritatis*, the council's Decree on the Adaptation and Renewal of Religious Life,[1] invited religious women and men to open the windows of their monasteries and convents to become deeply engaged in the world, the resounding "yes" by many communities came as simply the next step in their communal journey. What made this possible for so many United States women's religious communities is well documented and invaluable background reading for understanding the common dynamics operative across the communities. See, for example, *Nuns to Sisters: An Expanding Vocation*[2] and *Transformation of American Catholic Sisters (Women in the Political Economy)*.[3]

This book shares the stories of the journeys of members of one religious order, the Society of the Sacred Heart of Jesus in the United States. Always remaining grounded in prayer, the Society navigated the sometimes difficult transition from the semi-cloistered life to living in the outside world as they got closer to the people of God. As part of its renewal, the Society explored new ways to engage its historic apostolic work of education and experimented with new ministries, all in response to the council's call to engage more deeply with people pushed to the margins by unjust systems and structures.

The visionary leadership of Mother Sabine de Valon, RSCJ, the Society's superior general at the time of Vatican II, allowed the community to change almost everything, from how the religious lived; to how, where, and to whom they ministered; to how the Society operated internally; to how it governed itself. They grew into participatory leadership and governance while they explored the justice implications of all aspects of their community life. Grounded in those relationships, Society members answered calls to work for structural change here in the United States and throughout the world: at the local, national, and international levels; as activists, advocates, lobbyists, peacebuilders, and more.

The Society's changes in the five decades since Vatican II are, and continue to be, nothing short of transfiguring. What is remarkable as we make our way through the chapters is how seemingly gently this transfiguration unfolded, even when faced with resistance from inside and outside the Society. One author calls it a quiet revolution. I could not agree more. From working among them and other sisters like them, I know this revolution is possible only because of the depth of their individual and community formation, the strength of their commitment to one another and to the world, and their openness to the Heart of God. From this wellspring, the Society has proceeded, and still does today: systematically; year in and year out; always in discernment; always committed to service to a living, breathing, always evolving Body of Christ.

As the Second Vatican Council's reception continues to unfold in the universal Church today, concrete examples like this one of the Society of the Sacred Heart in the United States serve to expand our imaginations, animate our hopes and dreams, and provide important sources of inspiration. For me personally, learning about journeys like that of the Society has been a source of great life and love as I have discerned my own "yeses" in answer to the council's universal call to holiness. And while my specific formation, experience, and context have guided me to look for inspiration from women religious primarily in the United States,[4] these stories of women religious embracing Vatican II are everywhere in the Church in the world.

We hear echoes of the Society's journey each time we listen to Pope Francis talk about Vatican II, the culture of encounter, a synodal, listening Church. The Society of the Sacred Heart in the United States has graced us with just one example of how to embody these calls. May the quiet revolution continue, not only in traditional religious life, but also in all of us, the People of God, responding to the universal call to holiness in our lives and ministries.

Mary J. Novak
Executive Director, NETWORK Lobby for Catholic Social Justice
Associate, Congregation of St. Joseph.

The Way We Were: Life Before Vatican II

Many orders have been able to develop the core-spirit of their foundress to meet modern demands—to create flexible structures which are not frozen in past patterns but are open to experiment in response to changing needs. All this represents a breakthrough both for the nuns and for the Church.

Patricia Barrett, RSCJ
"Nuns in the Inner City,"
in Sister M. Charles Borromeo, CSC, ed. *The New Nuns*[5]

Like the position of women in society generally, religious life for women in the Catholic Church has been gradually evolving. For centuries, religious women's lifestyle was controlled by clergy, whether bishops or the pope himself. A major feature was enclosure, or cloister, the rule that confined the women to a single convent or monastery and forbade secular persons from entering the nuns' residence. By the time the Society of the Sacred Heart, the subject of this book, was founded in France in 1800, cloister was beginning to be less restrictive. Sisters in the newer religious orders moved from place to place, allowing them to engage in apostolic work, though usually this work was carried on within the confines of the house, or convent. Members of the Society of the Sacred Heart lived under this kind of cloister, often called semi-cloister; that is, they did not leave the convent property except for health care or other serious reasons, and schools were situated in the convent. The religious could, however, be sent from one convent to another to serve specific needs. Changes in these rules after the Second Vatican Council made possible the kind of work discussed in the chapters of this book

The Society originated in the wake of the French Revolution to contribute to the revival of church life, chiefly devotion to the Heart of Jesus, and founder Madeleine Sophie Barat chose the education of girls and young women as the primary ministry. The mission appealed to many young women, and the Society grew rapidly. After only eighteen years, even before it was approved by the Vatican, it spread to North America, and by the Second Vatican Council, it was established in many parts of the world.

The members of the Society of the Sacred Heart of Jesus called themselves Religious of the Sacred Heart, or RSCJ. They used family names and signed RSCJ. The initials stand for Religious of the Sacred Heart of Jesus in Latin, French and other languages. The same initials are used in all the countries where the Society operates. Religious of the Sacred Heart used to be divided into two classes: "choir nuns," called Mother, and coadjutrix sisters, called Sister. Since the merger of the two classes in 1964, all members of the Society are called Sister.

Most houses were on a fairly large property with a garden for outdoor exercise. And of course, there were playing fields for the students, which the sisters could also use. They wore the costume of the congregation, called the "habit." Normally, each RSCJ had a small room in the cloister, the part of the building used only by the religious. They followed a common schedule, "the order of day," took their meals together in silence, each having her assigned place in the refectory, or dining room. The day began with an hour of private mental prayer, Mass together in the chapel, the chanting of the office, a version of the official prayer of the Church. The chanting of the office took place also in the afternoon and evening.

Twice a day there was a half hour of recreation—that is, conversation directed by the superior—during which the sisters did needlework. The time between the prescribed prayers and meetings was filled with school duties or other work necessary for the running of the house and school. Sisters kept silence among themselves except for discussion related to work. They did not socialize with people outside the convent. Their families could visit once a month; they wrote to their parents once a month, if their parents were still living. They did not visit them nor take part in family events like weddings and funerals except by letter.

In the 1960s, when the Second Vatican Council told religious congregations to examine their rules and bring them up to date, the Society of the Sacred Heart held what is called a chapter, a representative legislative body. This group met in 1967 and completely revised the way of life just described. The new orientations, as they were called, allowed for a large measure of individual freedom and individual responsibility for one's life of prayer, work and leisure. Sisters were no longer restricted as to going out, visiting families, associating with people outside the congregation. These changes led to questions about what was suitable for religious: for example, forms of recreation; style of dress, as the traditional habit was given up; spending money. Some people who had entered straight from their family homes were ill-prepared to make wise decisions along these lines, and older religious sometimes disapproved of some of the choices of the younger members. In short, given the diversity of backgrounds and ages, they all had to learn how to get along and build community. For some people, the new lifestyle was not congenial; it was not what they had entered for, and they left. Others welcomed the personal freedom and responsibility it allowed for their lives and choices of work.

As noted above, the Society from the beginning had chosen education as the means by which it carried out its mission in the Church. Because of the requirements of cloister, that education had to be situated in the convents. Now a broader outreach was possible; sisters could go out to other institutions or work in different kinds of educational settings. They came to see that education was broader than schooling; it could take place in city neighborhoods, in clinics and social centers, for example. In this way, the places and types of educational ministry gradually diversified.

The early stages of this evolution form the subject of the chapters in this book. These significant changes have given rise to ongoing reflection among religious about their work and its relevance to the needs of contemporary society. This reflection has resulted in new understandings of their vocation; it has brought about a refounding of the Society in response to the calls of the Church and the world.

Vatican II & the Society of the Sacred Heart

Introduction

In January 1964, after the second session of the Second Vatican Council had concluded in December, Sabine de Valon, RSCJ, then superior general of the Society of the Sacred Heart of Jesus, wrote in a letter to her sisters:

> Yes, hope is certainly the virtue of the hour; our gaze is straining Godward; it is straining toward the future; something is coming to birth in the world, under the influence of grace; a star is shining in the night, the dawn is close at hand; we are awaiting the "tomorrow" that Love is preparing; tomorrow God will show his wonderful mercy and the eternal youth of his Church. It is the atmosphere of the Council that has raised this hope on the horizon; we do not yet know very much about its labors; we feel that they will be accomplished, no doubt under the sign of the Cross; but the Cross is good, and through it, the Holy Spirit is at work in the Church and in the world and will be able to renew the face of the earth.[6]

Mother de Valon sensed the Spirit's presence and the gift of hope in this profound moment in the Church, even as she saw that there were challenges ahead and much still to be done and recognizing the work would also be done under the "sign of the cross." The decades that followed would show that she was correct on all counts.

The story of the Religious of the Sacred Heart in the decades following Vatican II has much in common with that of many congregations of women religious. At the same time, each congregation has its own story of how it navigated this period. The same can also be said of how each region of the world in which the RSCJ lived and ministered responded to the council's calls. The contexts of Church and society in each area have also been significant influences in the reception of Vatican II in religious life.

The subsequent chapters of this anthology will illustrate what some of the movements of the Spirit looked like in the United States and Canada in the two decades following Vatican II. This chapter will first briefly offer some background on Vatican II so that the reader has a sense of what was occurring at this time.[7] It will then focus on some particular implications of the council for religious life. Finally, it will offer a larger context of the period before, during, and immediately after Vatican II through the lens of the Society of the Sacred Heart of Jesus from 1958 to 1967, the years of Sabine de Valon's leadership as superior general.

It is possible to get a glimpse into the complexities and challenges the Religious of the Sacred Heart faced in this era by examining the shifts in understandings of ministry, leadership (governance) and formation of new members and how these shifts were navigated by the Society and Superior General Sabine de Valon.

Vatican II: A Brief Sketch

On January 25, 1959, Pope John XXIII announced the twenty-first ecumenical council of the Roman Catholic Church. The Second Vatican Council, often referred to as Vatican II, was held in four sessions between 1962 and 1965 and produced sixteen major documents. The council would serve as a catalyst for a deepening and widening spiritual and pastoral response to the calls of the Spirit and would open up the Church even further to reading the signs of the times in order to better engage the world in which it lived and served.[8] In "The Pastoral Constitution on the Church in the Modern World" (*Gaudium et spes*), one of the later documents, we read how deeply the Church is to enter into the world: "The joys and the hopes, the griefs and the anxieties of the men [and women] of this age, especially those who are poor or in any way afflicted, these are the joys and hopes, the griefs and anxieties of the followers of Christ. Indeed, nothing genuinely human fails to raise an echo in their hearts."[9] The Church's leadership role is one that encourages and engages, and this can be done only by looking at the world and examining it with a lens from which to bring a faith tradition to responsive action.

Again, in *Gaudium et spes*:

> ... the Church seeks but a solitary goal: to carry forward the work of Christ under the lead of the befriending Spirit. And Christ entered this world to give witness to the truth, to rescue and not to sit in judgment, to serve and not to be served.
>
> To carry out such a task, the Church has always had the duty of scrutinizing the signs of the times and of interpreting them in the light of the Gospel. Thus, in language intelligible to each generation, she can respond to the perennial questions which men [and women] ask about this present life and the life to come, and about the relationship of the one to the other. We must therefore recognize and understand the world in which we live, its explanations, its longings, and its often dramatic characteristics.[10]

A clear servant leader image is called forth in this passage. The Spirit, who befriends us, leads us forward to a service that is responsive to the world in which we live. The Church, now with the dominant image of the "people of God,"[11] will respond best by going deeply into the reality and engaging it through the lens of the gospel call to love and justice.

Words often used to describe the movement of Vatican II are *aggiornamento* and *ressourcement*. *Aggiornamento* refers to renewing or bringing up to date elements of the Church in order to respond to the current moment. One example of this was the move to celebrate Eucharistic liturgy in the vernacular, the language of the local people, rather than in Latin. With this, Catholics could participate in their own language and celebrate more actively. *Ressourcement,* which means a return to the sources, was a call to depth. Those in religious life, for example, were asked to look more deeply into their earlier documents and histories to uncover key elements of their charism, history, and spirituality that were important for the congregation. Both words engaged people and institutions in a call to renewal and deepening of their faith lives.

The image of the people of God was a central part of the vision of Vatican II. All people have received a "universal call to holiness,"[12] meaning that every baptized person has a significant role to play in the Church. Before this, there was a hierarchy of importance that began with the pope and then moved down to cardinals, bishops, priests, deacons, brothers, women religious, and finally to the married and single persons. The call of the laity was meant to bring forth the gifts of all in the Church, even as roles are diverse. All are needed and all are important; all are called to holiness and relationship with God.

Another of the many gifts of this time is that all Catholics were encouraged to study Scripture. Before this the Bible was often left in some special place in a house or convent, but rarely read. The invitation to read Scripture opened up new questions and also opportunities for scholarship and reflection on the Word of God. The universal call to holiness also opened up the Church to dialogue with the world in a new way, one that saw and appreciated gifts in others, across faith traditions.

The renewal of religious life also came through *ressourcement* and *aggiornamento*. Religious congregations were asked to go back to their original sources to see how their wisdom might be applied to the changing times. As a result, congregations began exploring their earlier documents, reading earlier translations of their Constitutions and delving into their spiritual traditions. *Aggiornamento* meant that the ministries were looked at in light of the needs of the era. The purpose of particular congregational clothing ("habits") was looked at in terms of whether the need and witness were still present for some types of religious dress or whether different forms of dress would be more appropriate. Most of the external elements of religious life were looked at in light of purpose, witness, and need. Every question was valid. It was a time of great openness, a time of experimentation and freedom, to look at religious life in relation to the world and to discern to what the Spirit might be calling religious. It was also a time of considerable challenge, because what was once thought of as a stable and unchanging form of life was now called into question. These were turbulent and enriching times for religious.

It is also important to note that the changes brought forth by Vatican II did not begin with the opening of the council. While to some the council was a surprise, those hewing more closely to the theological and pastoral questions of the time recognized that the moment was ripe for renewal. Pope John XXIII sensed enough of the Spirit's stirrings to convoke the council in order to respond to the emerging calls.

Of course, every congregation and region of the world had its own way of responding to Vatican II. It is in looking more deeply at the story of the Religious of the Sacred Heart of Jesus around the time of Vatican II that we can perhaps better see the process, diversity of outreach, and way of living the gospel call to justice and peace in the context of that time.

Society of the Sacred Heart 1958-1967

As superior general, Mother de Valon had several experiences that influenced her vision and action toward renewal in the Society. She had led the congregation in significant missionary expansion, assisted in forming the international union of major superiors of women's congregations, and served as auditor during the third and fourth sessions of Vatican II. In addition, while some changes in the Society had occurred prior to the Second Vatican Council, changes implemented after the council, including understandings of ministry, participatory leadership models, and holistic religious formation processes, were far-reaching on local, provincial and international levels. All of this affected not only Society members, but also those with whom they ministered.[13]

Missionary Expansion

Mother de Valon's time was one of unusual missionary momentum resulting largely from her travels and the misery and poverty she witnessed. While the Society of the Sacred Heart had a strong missionary consciousness from its earliest days,[14] Mother de Valon's travels widened her commitment, prompting her to mobilize both the Religious of the Sacred Heart and the alumnae. Thirty-one foundations were made between 1958 and 1967. This expansion was a means of responding to the calls of the Church and the world. Requests came from alumnae and Church hierarchy for foundations in Sudan, Cambodia, Kenya, Ghana, Zambia, Fiji, Sweden, Portugal, and South America. The Society's leaders in Rome gave priority to requests from Asia and Africa in order to take advantage of opportunities offered by development occurring in those areas.[15]

Mother de Valon also initiated a new publication, called *Mitte me* [Send me],[16] the goal of which was "to spread the love of the Heart of Jesus throughout the world,"[17] as well as to educate and call forth conversation on essential questions in mission.

In addition, in 1962, Mother de Valon launched the "Missionary Volunteers of the Sacred Heart." These young women went to mission countries to help the Religious of the Sacred Heart, not to earn money, but to devote themselves to the educational and apostolic work in which the religious were engaged.[18] Records show that between 1962 and 1968, 146 young women from twenty-one countries ministered in Africa, Asia, and South America.[19] The works they took on were primarily to address unmet needs, in many cases, works in which the religious could not personally engage because of cloister.[20] It is important to note that the sisters did see the needs, some on their own and some because of the calls of the alumnae and the Church. As ensuing chapters will show, once cloister was lifted, the religious themselves also moved into these areas.

The nuns started foundations among the very needy. One example among many is from India:

> "In Bombay and Bangalore, the Sacred Heart was providing education to an elite who could supply professionals with a Christian spirit to a society in the midst of radical change."[21] On May 16, 1961, a foundation was established among the outcasts. Located in the Diocese of Poona, 300 kilometers from Bombay, Haregaon was a town whose population depended on a sugar plant that offered work only one month out of two. They [Jesuits] asked the Sacred Heart to take charge of a secondary school for girls.[22] In Haregaon, they lived among malnourished people who had only a strip of cloth tied at the waist for clothing: "Our children are so poor that they spontaneously put the bath towels we give them around their shoulders, having nothing else to protect themselves against the cold."[23]

Mother de Valon engaged the Sacred Heart family, particularly the alumnae, for she saw their capacities to change the situations of people who are poor and oppressed. She called on the alumnae's creativity and generosity as she sought to involve them in the Society's mission, "to utilize their ranks, their abilities and their resources." In Lima, Peru, she exhorted alumnae to mobilize to respond to illiteracy and poverty, as well as to teach the faith. In Lima, after visiting the Agustino section,[24] on April 20, 1965, she wrote to the alumnae a letter that would update and redirect their activities. "Not to know how to read, to know almost nothing of what can clarify thought, is a terrible evil; to know almost nothing of eternal life and of the ways that lead to it is a yet more horrible fate," her letter said.[25] Mother de Valon clearly saw the needs of those who lacked resources and whose very lives were vulnerable. However, for the religious themselves to respond to some of these needs brought up the question of cloister. Up to this time as we have seen, the Society lived what was described as a semi-cloistered life. That meant that people came to the religious, generally for education, rather than the religious going out to the people. In addition, the prayer and community schedule functioned on a quasi-monastic structure.

Mother de Valon knew that new ministries connected to the unmet needs would only be advocated for and possible if the rules around cloister changed. Around this same time, one of the commissions of Vatican II charged with renewal in religious life was looking at how congregations described themselves. The council's "Decree on the Adaptation and Renewal of Religious Life," *Perfectae Caritatis,* stated:

> In these [apostolic] communities, apostolic and charitable activity belongs to the very nature of the religious life, seeing that it is a holy service and a work characteristic of love, entrusted to them by the Church to be carried out in its name. These communities, then, should adjust their rules and customs to fit the demands of the apostolate to which they are dedicated. The fact however that apostolic religious life takes on many forms requires that its adaptation and renewal take account of this diversity and provide that the lives of religious dedicated to the service of Christ in these various communities be sustained by special provisions appropriate to each.

It was obvious that the Society, "while based on prayer and the interior life,"[26] was an apostolic congregation and had been so from the beginning. The first task the founder and her companions undertook was to operate a boarding school for girls. This was followed within weeks by a free school for working class girls. These two educational ministries constituted the Society's chief apostolic work. The challenge now was to accept and embody in the Society's rules and way of life the demands of the apostolate. Cloister had already been abrogated at the Society's General Chapter of 1964. In light of what was going to be said in *Perfectae Caritatis*, that apostolic religious should be exempt from cloister, the general chapter enacted more flexible rules. It now remained to choose how to adapt further to apostolic requirements.

In reality, some of the choosing was already happening. For example, in Chad, in 1964, while cloister was still being strictly observed in the whole Society, at one point, under pressure from a priest, some of the sisters went to one of the villages to attend midnight Mass. The experience gave the religious a better understanding of the families of their students and the realities of village life.[27]

The emphasis on understanding and adapting to the demands of the Society's apostolic identity that evolved from Vatican II had significant implications for the ministries and the relationships of the religious. The understanding of the Society of the Sacred Heart as a congregation[28] of apostolic life in 1967 was a shift to be underscored. Luirard writes that "Defining itself as a congregation of apostolic life, the Society of the Sacred Heart took as its starting point social needs, which varied from country to country. In light of this diversity, a government had to be worked out to make possible service to the Church."[29] As stated in the documents of Special Chapter 1967:

> Consecrated as we are to education, ours is an apostolic institute whose life has its source in intimate union with Christ and serves "Christ himself in his members." Love of the Incarnate Word must inspire not only our life but its structure, and these should be oriented to our service in the apostolate.
>
> One of the duties of the chapter is to remove anything that prevents our responding effectively to the call of the Church . . . . Once the Church has trusted us with the work of education, we must respond by giving an individual and collective witness to justice, authenticity, freedom and love.
>
> We want to face facts: two-thirds of the world goes hungry; two hundred fifty million children lack education; the promotion of women poses its own problems. We must extend our apostolate to include all social classes.[30]

Removing enclosure was a significant step toward bringing the religious closer to the experiences of the persons on the margins struggling for justice. A further significance of this moment that cannot be overstated is that the movement out of cloister affected not only ministry, but the very life of the Society at its heart. Prayer and cultivation of the interior life are essential calls for Religious of the Sacred Heart, and Mother de Valon rightly saw cloister as instrumental in fostering a life of prayer. It fell to Mother de Valon as superior general to help the Society to negotiate the shift from a cloistered life to a way of engaging with the world, while preserving the centrality of a life rooted in prayer.

From the 1964 chapter directives and decisions comes a well-known Society quote that speaks volumes to the shifting in motion: "Our enclosure, until now, has been the guardian of our vows. Now, it is our vows that will safeguard our spirit of enclosure."[31] What was required in the midst of this? Positive, theological language for the vows, community and ministry—in sum, for all aspects of religious life. And a spirit of discernment for nuns experiencing calls to new ministries. Consequently, it was a formidable task for Mother de Valon to try as she did to preserve the experience of the past, to maintain the unity of the whole, and to respond to the Vatican Council's calls.

Leadership and Governance

It is helpful to see some of the background and context from which Mother de Valon looked at questions of religious life at this pivotal time.

At the end of 1962, and at the request of Pope John XXIII, Mother de Valon was instrumental in the formation of an international union of general superiors of women's congregations along the model of the one for men. She was named a councilor on the first leadership team of what came to be known as the International Union of Superiors General (UISG). Luirard explains that

> In this position she became an auditor during the third session of the Council. There were fifteen women auditors, eight of whom were religious.[32] Mother de Valon was named "head of the women auditors on September 25, 1964 . . . . She valued the mission confided to her . . . worked on the texts with the other superiors general and strengthened relations with experts and with conciliar Fathers from all over the world. The motherhouse served as a meeting place for some of the bishops. Mother de Valon thus reinforced her sense of the Church and her conviction that it was in Rome that modernization of ecclesial communities could be effected. Knowing what the Church thought was invaluable.[33]

This was a tremendous honor and gave Mother de Valon deep insight into the thinking of the conciliar members. She had a sense of the global and dynamic ecclesial thinking. However, these insights and the movements of the time also had costs. As Frances Gimber, RSCJ, noted in her biography of Mother Marie Louise Schroen, RSCJ, Mother de Valon's participation in the work of the council, though gratifying,

> was a source of deep anxiety and pain to her. She saw that she was going to have to initiate significant changes in the way of life of her religious as a result of some of the Council's decisions . . . . Mother de Valon heard in the debate on the Council floor denials of everything she had ever believed about religious life and the Society's particular understanding of it, which involved cloister, separation from the world, silence, and a number of other monastic practices. These had as their purpose to safeguard the contemplative life of the religious, but they resulted in the diminution of their apostolic effectiveness. The Council decreed that religious congregations were to define themselves as either apostolic or contemplative and then adjust their lifestyles accordingly. It seemed evident that the Society of the Sacred Heart belonged in the apostolic category but the consequences of recognizing that reality were far from clear or acceptable to everyone.[34]

Another major area of change was related to growing demands to establish equality among the Society's members: that is, dissolving the coadjutrix sister category. From medieval times, in most religious orders, there were two classes of nuns, corresponding to classes in society in general. Lay or coadjutrix sisters performed domestic and rural work, and choir nuns recited the Office in choir, did the teaching or other intellectual work, and were responsible for the government of the houses and the congregation as a whole. Now there would be one class of Religious of the Sacred Heart of Jesus.[35] This shift had begun already in 1958, albeit slowly.[36] In 1960, Mother de Valon proposed the same habit for everyone. It was accepted.[37] Four years later, the distinction between choir nun and coadjutrix sister was officially dissolved in the General Chapter of 1964.

Once those two key changes had been made—suppressing cloister and dissolving the coadjutrix sister category—Mother de Valon had to deal with even more calls for greater inclusion and equality. Governance structures had to shift in order to effect greater decentralization in the spirit of Vatican II. In 1967, as a result of consultations with the membership, significant changes in governance structures took place, along with an evolution in the spirit of governance. Note the principles of Catholic social thought inherent in the changes:

> The principles of subsidiarity, decentralization, co-responsibility and participation were presented as means of fostering growth, responsibility in obedience, adaptation to the new rhythms of life of the times, collective projects and consultation; for responsibilities would be shared "in spite of the risk of error." Common problems would have to be studied together: order of day, religious discipline, community life, our current and possibly new works and the financial situation.[38]

Responding to any concerns that these new ways were not in the earliest Constitutions, the Orientations of Special Chapter 1967 reminded all that these movements were in the spirit of the Society's founder, Saint Madeleine Sophie Barat, and had been implied in her thought, and thus had authority.[39]

Some changes in structures specified in the 1967 Special Chapter documents can be summarized as follows: Provinces replaced vicariates. Superiors were to be named after consultation with the religious. The length of their term was limited. Councils were created at every level. Their functions, their composition, the frequency of meetings were all defined.[40]

Notice the shifting of more authority to the local level, with religious being asked for their opinions. Utilizing the gifts of more people in the service of leadership is also evident here, for prior to this, some who were named superiors could be so for life. Now there would be a greater flow of persons between external ministry and internal ministry. General chapters would no longer elect a superior general for life.... Sharing authority was now viewed as important.[41]

A key point to note here is that the priority of prayer continued amid this new identification of the Religious of the Sacred Heart as apostolic women. This offers us a key to navigating shifts in our own time and in the future. In the

Orientations we see the reference to the Society's original Constitutions, which state that the Society's mission and ministries are "founded on prayer and the interior life,"

> The special chapter underlined the apostolic character of prayer, from which "no one can dispense us, because no one can dispense us from God." However, it said that "there are countless ways to pray, according to people, times, and life's challenges. God speaks to each one in an individual manner; the response must be personal and searching."[42]

Considering how much change would happen in the decades to follow, this was a crucial statement. It preserved the key elements of religious life—prayer, community and ministry—even as the ways in which these are lived would continue to evolve.

Formation and Implications for Ministry

Yet another area of shifts that happened in the Society around the time of Vatican II is related to formation of new members.

First, an international novitiate in Italy was opened in January 1964. As a result of visits to Asia, Mother de Valon "thought of introducing the essential elements of missiology at the beginning of formation, in particular in the international novitiate, opened in Italy at Frascati, that she hoped would nourish the missions."[43] One may also see in her initiatives how Mother de Valon's experiences among people living in poverty continued to move her efforts to lead the Society's members, in their individual, communal, prayer and ministerial lives, toward a deeper response to the realities of those on the margins. These efforts and calls continued to move RSCJ in the decades to come.

Second, adaptability to change became a criterion for new members. Responding to the signs of the times, as signaled by Vatican II, that is, to the needs of society and the Church, was to be crucial to religious life and ministry after Vatican II. A number of people saw change coming, and probanists (those preparing for final profession in the Society) were told to be open to change or to leave.

Third, education for the Religious of the Sacred Heart shifted after 1964, opening up more areas of study. Young religious were required to undertake studies in theology during the two years following their first vows. In addition, emphasis was placed on preparation for the missions. The Special Chapter 1967 highlighted the movement toward what we now call interculturality, especially for those going to the missions. In order to serve well, a missionary must

> be persuaded that one has much to learn from those whom one comes to evangelize; to wish at any cost to understand them in their language; to be ready to change habits in the areas of well-being, food, lodging, liturgical adaptation; to be happy to do without many things in the material,

> intellectual, artistic and spiritual realms; to know how to leave aside one's own patriotism and to understand political questions with the frame of mind of the people of the country.[44]

We find here a deep desire toward what could now be described as a conversion toward becoming an intercultural community, within the local community and within the wider culture within which one lives, prays and ministers. Language learning was seen as indispensable. It is quite touching to read that:

> Our efforts [to master the local languages] will prove to the inhabitants of the country that we do not love them only "for the love of God," but for themselves, as they are. In the eyes of God they are God's children the same as we are, therefore our equals, as rich as we in God's eyes, and having the same divine and human value. To believe therefore in their value, their qualities, to respect them. In coming to them we have as much to receive as to give them.[45]

This understanding, recognizing each person's inherent dignity, would be essential in moving forward toward ensuring justice and peace for each and all.

Conclusion

In the decades following Vatican II, the Society was transformed. RSCJ were deeply affected by the calls to greater mutuality in leadership, sharing of authority, removing distinctions among members, efforts toward intercultural living, and ongoing adaptability to the signs of the times.

All of these areas of change were very much linked to the ministries that would follow, whether those were direct service in education in Sacred Heart schools, or other forms of education, including accompaniment, social service, and work for social justice. As the 1971 Synod of Bishops stated: "Action on behalf of justice and participation in the transformation of the world fully appear to us as a constitutive dimension of the preaching of the gospel, or, in other words, of the Church's mission for the redemption of the human race and its liberation from every oppressive situation."[46]

Readers will see in the chapters that follow the myriad ways in which the Society has evolved in response to the signs of the times during and well beyond the era of Vatican II. We are now in the time of Pope Francis, one who lived the renewal of Vatican II and is again calling the Church to deeper renewal. Who knows what this renewal will look like? But we can be certain that the Spirit is leading and that those of us in religious life are once again asked to respond to the cries of the people and cries of the earth as we seek to bring about the reign of God. And we can consider what the adaptations in the years after Vatican II might teach us about navigating the massive shifts in our own time.

So we go, together!

New Roles for Women After Vatican II

Introduction

The Second Vatican Council launched a quiet revolution among women in the Church, not because of a particular document that was issued but because a spirit and a mission pervaded the whole event, gradually inspiring the recognition among women of the gifts they had been given for the sake of the people of God. Traditional male, and generally clerical, roles—seminary teaching, retreats and spiritual direction, and parish and diocesan leadership—began to be filled by competent, well-trained women. These new ministries, assumed by Religious of the Sacred Heart in the ensuing years, are the focus of this chapter.

First, a word about the context that called forth this flowering of new ministries. Opposite forces were pulling at the Catholic imagination in the 1960s. On the one hand, these years represented one of the most turbulent and discordant decades in world history, marked in the United States by the civil rights movement, the Vietnam War and mounting anti-war protests, political assassinations, including that of the first Roman Catholic in the White House, and the growing chasm of values among generations.

On the other hand, for those attentive to the drama playing out in Rome, renewal was in the air. The Vatican Council identified itself with the joys and hopes, the griefs and anxieties of all peoples, especially the poor and afflicted—all of humankind on a journey together, fostering the reign of God. The council issued a universal call to holiness, and it declared the full participation of the laity in the Church's pastoral mission. The renewed liturgy, with its emphasis on "full, conscious and active participation," was a perfect symbol of the burgeoning empowerment of all Catholics in the life of the Church, in the spirit of the council.

Several Society initiatives influenced an expansion of RSCJ ministries. The Special Chapter 1967 was convened by the Society of the Sacred Heart shortly after the close of Vatican II to attempt to align the Society with the chief teachings of the council. There followed a regular general chapter in 1970 that continued that process. A new vocabulary came into play: renewal, decentralization, adaptations, participation, pluriformity, collegiality, subsidiarity, options. During these years immediately following Vatican II, the Society adjusted as best it could to the spirit of the council and made decisions related to the adaptations called for in religious life. There was more autonomy, more personal authority, more attention to relationships and to personal growth and the professional development of each member. Large institutional living gradually gave way to small groups, communities, living in a homelike atmosphere. There was an end to the rule of silence and an end to cloister.

Perhaps most significant in the flourishing of some new ministries in the 1970s was a decision that had been taken at the Society's General Chapter of 1964. At that chapter, and in accordance with the directives of the Sacred Congregation for Religious, the Society adopted a two-year period of doctrinal formation after first vows. This formation included a solid initiation into Scripture, a serious and consecutive study of dogmatic and moral theology, some elements of philosophy, and a history of the present life of the Church. The aim of doctrinal formation, according to the acts of the chapter, was to form aspirants[47] in "a deep interior life, religious maturity, stability, and the practice of the virtues—solid habits to last a lifetime." This decision played out in a variety of ways across the world. In the United States, young RSCJ were clustered together in each of the five provinces for study. This produced a cadre of young religious steeped in biblical studies and theology. For many of these aspirants, doctrinal formation played a decisive role in their future ministerial discernments. Carolyn Osiek, RSCJ, is a case in point.

Seminary Education

After Sister Osiek made her first vows in 1965, she was sent to Manhattanville College of the Sacred Heart in Purchase, New York, for her doctrinal formation, joining a group of New York aspirants pursuing masters' degrees in teaching religious studies. Among her classes, Sister Osiek took a course from Kathyrn Sullivan, RSCJ, an extraordinary biblical scholar and teacher. Sister Osiek was hooked. In 1968, she was directed to do further graduate studies. Her provincial, Elizabeth Cavanagh, RSCJ, favored a degree in educational administration that would prepare her for a versatile ministry at both the academy and college levels. But when asked, Sister Osiek said her preference was biblical studies.

Within the next two years, Sister Osiek moved to Boston and was accepted into the doctoral program in New Testament and Christian Origins at Harvard Divinity School. As she began the program in 1970, her provincial told her that this was the first time the province had sent someone for doctoral study without the goal of meeting a specific need in one of the Society's colleges. That also meant that Sister Osiek would have to search for employment when her studies neared completion. She was not the first in higher education to be employed outside Society institutions, but it was still a fairly new practice when, in 1977, she accepted a position at the Catholic Theological Union in Chicago (CTU). CTU was a place that became, and remains to this day, a mecca for Religious of the Sacred Heart, whether as faculty members or as full- or part-time students at all stages of religious life, including, most recently, those in initial formation.

Indeed, Catholic Theological Union was a splendid choice. It was founded in 1968 by three religious orders of men (the Passionists, Franciscans, and Servites) who, inspired by Vatican II, desired to move their formation programs to an urban center, near a major university—in this case, the University of Chicago—and close to theologates of other Christian denominations to make cross-registration possible. Other religious orders joined them in rapid succession (CTU is currently sponsored by twenty-four religious congregations), and when Sister Osiek arrived, she found an international group of students, motivated men and women, who would eventually serve all over the world in a variety of pastoral situations. CTU counts among its graduates scholars, bishops, superiors general and so many others doing significant ministry in all parts of the globe. It also claims three martyrs.

Kathleen Hughes, RSCJ, joined Sister Osiek at CTU in the fall of 1980, accepting a teaching position in the Department of Word and Worship after completing doctoral studies with a specialization in liturgy at the University of Notre Dame. Like Sister Osiek, Sister Hughes had been given permission to pursue specialized studies in an academic discipline for which there were no position openings in Society schools. The studies committee of the Society's Boston-based Washington Province recognized and blessed her study of liturgy "as a preparation for service in the American Church."

Barbara Bowe, RSCJ, was the third of the Society to accept a faculty appointment at CTU after teaching for three years at the Maryhill School of Theology in the Philippines. Like Sister Osiek, she had studied at the Harvard Divinity School in the Department of New Testament and Christian Origins. She served at CTU for twenty years before her untimely death of a brain tumor in 2010, after having just completed the book she had always wanted to write, *Biblical Foundations of Spirituality: Touching A Finger to the Flame.*[48]

Over the years, CTU has attracted many Religious of the Sacred Heart. Rosemary (Ronnie) Dewey, RSCJ, came to CTU on sabbatical after completing her work as provincial in 1982 and stayed on as administrative assistant to the president, Jack Linnan, CSV. In the same year, Mary Bernstein, RSCJ, was hired as business manager. In 1990, Barbara Quinn stayed in the RSCJ community at CTU for three years while in the process of transferring to the Society from another religious congregation, the Grey Nuns of the Sacred Heart. Mary Frohlich joined the faculty in 1993, developing a rich set of offerings in spirituality and designing a doctor of ministry degree in that discipline. After eight years, and having explored several congregations of women religious, Mary Frohlich entered the Society of the Sacred Heart. After completing her transfer, Sister Quinn returned to CTU and completed a doctor of ministry degree in spirituality under the guidance of Sister Frohlich. Mary Charlotte Chandler, RSCJ, came to CTU in 2002 from the Center for Applied Research in the Apostolate (CARA), where she had served as director of the Center for the Study of Religious Life. Next, Maria Cimperman, RSCJ, accepted a position teaching Catholic Theological Ethics and directing the Center for the Study of Consecrated Life. In the fall of 2017, the Society established an international English-speaking novitiate, taking advantage of the global population, and began welcoming novices from the United States, Korea and Japan.

It was a propitious choice that Sister Osiek made back in 1977!

While Catholic Theological Union became a mecca for a number of newly-minted RSCJ scholars and for RSCJ students of all ages, it was only one of numerous places where RSCJ were drawn to seminary education as their ministerial focus. Weston School of Theology in Boston, (now the School of Theology and Ministry at Boston College), welcomed Nancy Kehoe, RSCJ, as director of field education and Gail O'Donnell, RSCJ, as director of continuing education and spiritual formation for mission. Theresa Monroe, RSCJ, taught canon law and leadership studies, and Sister Quinn, spiritual formation. Ann Johnston, RSCJ, took an ecumenical route; she taught Hebrew Scripture at the ecumenical Bangor Theological Seminary in Maine. Mary McGann, RSCJ, a student of both ethno-musicology and liturgical studies, completed her doctoral work in the Graduate Theological Union (GTU) in Berkeley, California and joined the faculty at one of its member schools, the Franciscan School of Theology. Annice Callahan, RSCJ, accepted a faculty appointment at Regis, the Jesuit Theologate in Toronto, after teaching briefly at the Sacred Heart School of Theology in Hales Corners, Wisconsin. Her work, Karl Rahner's *Spirituality of the Pierced Heart,*[49] was enormously enriched by frequent conversations with Rahner himself during her seven months of research in Austria.

What was the attraction to seminary education for all of these women? Some answers seem obvious: a desire to teach at the graduate level and work with a vital group of colleagues and a diverse student body; the possibility of combining scholarship and pastoral interests; the opportunity to offer a wide range of courses and develop personal scholarly attractions through graduate seminars; and the vibrant sense of serving the Church.

Two other reasons were perhaps most compelling. For one, seminary education offers the possibility of "the multiplier effect" in training priests and pastoral ministers for service both locally and for the world Church. In the course of the seminary curriculum, the faculty exercises a profound influence on the students, on their theological grounding, their values, their pastoral judgment. For example, when Sister Hughes expressed surprise to a colleague after having received several term papers from priesthood candidates who referred to the priest as "he or she," she categorically denied ever having raised the question of women's ordination. Her colleague replied: "But of course you did. You were standing in front of them." These graduates, in turn, have exercised the same multiplier influence in every community they serve.

Perhaps the greatest attraction to seminary education, especially at places like CTU and Jesuit theologates, was that it was thoroughly exhilarating to be among colleagues who delighted in exploring the broad and timely issues that had surfaced in the wake of the council: interreligious dialogue, economic justice, war and peace, the explosion of lay ministries, the formation and development of personal conscience, issues around the language of prayer and ways of addressing God, the growing concern for ecology and an ecological spirituality, sexual ethics. Writing, teaching, preaching, faculty seminars, lunch conversations—all were collaborative and stimulating. There was a real sense that a new Church was being born.

At CTU, Sister Osiek stirred the conversational pot with the publication of *Beyond Anger*, a book in the making for about three years as she worked out for herself how to live through the awareness of the marginalization and mistreatment of women in the Church and turn that awareness into something creative. It was said of this book: "Our author encourages embracing the cross, not as passive victims, but as free agents capable of sustaining the liberating and redemptive suffering that is necessary in order that women's continuing presence in the Church can effect needed changes according to the pattern of the gospel."[50] This book had a wide readership and enormous influence. It certainly stoked the fires among feminists interested in wider roles for women in the post-Vatican II Church.

Houses of Prayer, Retreats and Spiritual Direction

Perhaps the most obvious of "new ministries" was actually among the oldest of the Society's ministries—that of supporting and sustaining a life of prayer and encouraging the spiritual growth of others. Retreats "offered to persons living in the world" was one of the four means identified by Madeleine Sophie Barat[51] in the *Constitutions* of 1815 "for the purpose of glorifying the Sacred Heart of Jesus by laboring for the sanctification of others." Moreover, Madeleine Sophie had a vision of a "great throng of adorers"—students, colleagues, families and friends—whose contemplative life would be nurtured by her sisters. This ministry was exercised differently across the provinces but generally included hosting occasional retreats for women, preached by Jesuits, and innumerable "heart talks" with visitors in the parlor.

Two significant developments, one external and one internal, influenced the interest among RSCJ in spiritual direction, retreats, and houses of prayer after the council.

The external influence was the retrieval, among the Jesuits, of the directed retreat according to the genius of their founder, Saint Ignatius Loyola. In the late 1960s, a number of North American Jesuits made their tertianship[52] at St. Beuno's in Wales, where there was interest in and experimentation with the recovery of the model of directed retreats enshrined in the Spiritual Exercises of Ignatius. These men, including such luminaries as Fathers John English, David Fleming, William Barry, and George Schemel, returned to their provinces and initiated directed retreats. This renewed interest in the Spiritual Exercises has been described as a confluence of grace that became incarnate during the late 1960s and early 1970s in North America. It launched other related breakthroughs, among them inviting and training non-Jesuit women and men to become spiritual directors and retreat-givers alongside their Jesuit friends.

Meanwhile, in the late 1960s, newly formed small communities of RSCJ were searching for ways to pray together. The Little Office of Our Lady had been recited daily, but what was needed were patterns of prayer more conducive to nourishing life together in small groups. A variety of practices emerged: reflection on the Scriptures of the day, guided meditation, sitting together in silence, centering prayer, periodic days of renewal. There was also a need to discover and incorporate music that could function in the renewed liturgy and also act as the sound track of our spiritual lives. And there was a desire for training in spiritual direction and in leadership roles in liturgy in order to open up the Word of God, to articulate the hopes and needs in all our hearts, to share with others the background and tools to enable them to engage in their own biblical exploration and so deepen their knowledge and love of the Word of God. Above all, there was a desire to have the tools to meet the deep spiritual hungers in our students, colleagues, and friends. Houses of prayer were born of just such longing.

Ephpheta House

Ephpheta House of Prayer in Detroit was one such response. It was begun in community discernment at the Academy of the Sacred Heart in Bloomfield Hills, Michigan. Drawing on the directives of Special Chapter 1967, several in the community explored the need for a new expression of the spirit of the Society of the Sacred Heart that would be concretized by a ministry of prayer. They articulated their discernment by saying: Prayer has always been central to the spirit of the Society; our life of prayer and of apostolic activity is meant to be one; there is the need of this service of the Church to the world; we have been encouraged to undertake new ventures; we have been encouraged to share such new ventures with others.

By 1970 Sister McGann and Nancy Murphy, RSCJ, realized they both shared a desire for such a ministry of spirituality. They joined forces with two Sisters of Charity, Sisters Pat McNally and Kay Tardiff, who were interested in a similar commitment. The preliminary purpose of these founders of Ephpheta House was to create an inter-congregational open community characterized by living simply and hospitably, providing retreats, scripture study, and prayer resources, and networking with other groups engaged in spiritual formation. Initially, the members occupied a house on the property of the Society's Bloomfield Hills academy for their community, but after two years, the group moved from there to the vacant convent of a parish in Auburn Heights, Michigan, where they doubled the space for overnight guests.

In 1973, the two Sisters of Charity were recalled to work among their own sisters. Meanwhile, Ephpheta House continued to attract seekers of the holy life, and other Religious of the Sacred Heart joined the community for at least a year: Sisters Oonah Ryan, Margo Morris, Frances Tobin, Neila Farias of the province of India, Mary Ellen Pohl, Rose Marie Quilter, and Barbara Bireley. The work of the community expanded to include classes in Scripture and in prayer for young people and adults, workshops for catechists, days of prayer for religious and lay people, liturgy preparation for various groups, and preparation of resource material for prayer. An enduring and beloved musical resource was produced at Ephpheta, a recording of original compositions by Sister McGann and Margo Morris, RSCJ, entitled *Walk Humbly with Your God*[53] To this day, RSCJ offer their prayers of gratitude to one another with a song from this same recording, Sister McGann's "I Thank My God for You."

In 1975, coinciding with Sister McGann's departure for preparation for profession, the Archdiocese of Detroit expressed an interest in basing the outreach of the sisters in two of its parishes. This seemed a wise development, and in 1976, Ephpheta House of Prayer closed.

Abba House of Prayer

Abba House of Prayer in Albany, New York, had a similar beginning. In 1971, several members of the community at Kenwood Academy of the Sacred Heart were drawn to the idea of a ministry of prayer and spirituality. For the first two years, the five founders of Abba House—Sisters Mabel Dorsey, Mary Parkinson. Rose Marie Quilter, Elizabeth Hoye and Mary Gen Smyth, all RSCJ—located their ministry in the Society's former novitiate on the Kenwood property. In 1973, the Society of the Sacred Heart purchased a house on Western Avenue in the city of Albany, and Sisters Hoye and Smyth moved to that location, a spacious fifteen-room house that was more central to the city. The ministry was quickly embraced by the people of Albany. On the occasion of the twenty-fifth anniversary of Abba House of Prayer, the co-directors were able to report that more than 20,000 people, as individuals or in groups, had come to Abba House for prayer, scripture classes, special programs, for quiet time, or to make a retreat.

The purpose and goals of Abba House had been clearly articulated from the beginning: to be a center of prayer, of praise and worship of God, and active intercession for the diocese, the Church, and the world; to be an open, contemplative house where all persons could grow in their own prayerfulness by experiencing the support of a praying community; to instruct others in prayer and the study of the Scriptures through Abba House offerings; to serve outside Abba House in various parishes; to pray for Christian unity and witness to it by frequent contact with those of various denominations; and to be a source of consciousness-raising for the advancement of peace and justice.

While Ephpheta House enjoyed close collaboration between two religious orders, a distinguishing characteristic of Abba House was its ecumenical thrust. It enjoyed collaboration with an Episcopalian retreat house, and an Episcopalian sister was part of the community. The Abba board of directors had Lutheran, Episcopalian and Presbyterian members. Ecumenical group meetings took place at Abba. Both Sisters Hoye and Smyth served on the ecumenical commission of the Albany diocese, and Sister Hoye was a diocesan representative to the area council of churches. Jewish and Buddhist believers were among Abba's guests, and a course in world religions was one of their regular offerings. Sisters Hoye and Smyth, the co-directors of Abba, were inspired by Vatican II's universal call to holiness and worked for nearly forty years to nurture its realization.

The Spiritual Ministry Center

Yet a third model of a house of prayer was established in San Diego in 1984 by three RSCJ: Mary Ann Foy, Betty Boyter, and Susan Campbell. The trio came to San Diego with rich backgrounds. Sister Foy had previously served as director of the permanent diaconate and director of ministries in the Diocese of Memphis. After a stint as assistant formation director for the Society, Sister Boyter had joined Sister Foy in Memphis as director of the family life office. Sister Campbell had served as director of formation for the Society's San Francisco Province and had just completed a year of spiritual renewal at CTU, taking courses in theology, scripture, liturgy and ethics. Sisters Foy and Boyter had a passion for lay spirituality, for finding ways to nourish the spiritual hunger among lay women and men. They hoped to develop a center of adult spirituality where they would train lay people for leadership within the Church. Sister Campbell was steeped in both Eastern and Western traditions of spirituality and was gifted as a spiritual guide, especially in working with individuals. The gifts and interests of this trio merged and allowed the development of a spiritual ministry team able to meet the broad range of requests they were soon to receive.

They had been encouraged to come to San Diego by RSCJ living there who regarded the city as something of a spiritual desert with few resources for a growing Catholic population. In point of fact, San Diego was the seventh largest city in the United States, and it had no retreat center. The vicar for religious in the San Diego diocese told them she could list only three spiritual directors in the area when asked for referrals.

For three years, Sisters Foy, Boyter, and Campbell lived and worked in the Tecolote area of San Diego. They had been advised by the local bishop, Bishop Leo Maher, to begin cautiously by introducing themselves to the local clergy and winning the approval and support of this key constituency. Their ministry was established through these parish contacts and their repertoire grew: a year-long engagement for talks on spirituality in one parish; evening sessions on different aspects of discipleship in another; a women's retreat focused on "pondering the Word with Mary"; a development of presentations for the diocese as a whole.

They described themselves thus: "We began as a group of three Religious of the Sacred Heart with a desire to share with others our gifts and strivings for mutual growth. We were committed to fostering the spiritual and apostolic growth of the men and women of our world. We offered retreats, workshops, and programs in the Christian tradition of presentation, reflection and discernment."

After three years, and with growing interest in their spiritual offerings, the trio moved to their permanent location in the city's Ocean Beach area. This new space provided a home for more opportunities for spiritual direction and overnight accommodations for those seeking weekend, eight-day, and thirty-day retreats. Over time, other RSCJ came to the center, and the gifts of these successive team members have expanded and diversified its offerings. It continues to thrive in San Diego to this day.

Service in the Church

It is so interesting to look back on the documents of the Society's Special Chapter 1967, just two years after the close of Vatican Council II. Education was and remained the way for Religious of the Sacred Heart to live out their charism of glorifying the Heart of Jesus, but the means had diversified. The chapter threw open the windows, to use a metaphor dear to Pope John XXIII, the convenor of the Vatican Council II, and threw open the doors as well, as it considered the broadest range possible of ways to exercise the service of education:

> In a world where the Church calls us to new tasks, we must give to education its full present-day dimensions. In addition to our educational institutes, primary and secondary schools, normal schools, university colleges, other means are in our power today: teaching in the parishes, in the inner-city, catechetical centers, student centers, classes in adult education, centers for the handicapped and for the abandoned, visits to families according to apostolic needs, vacation camps, participation in missionary teams; finally, every work of education as the need arises.[54]

Parishes all over the country were in need of volunteers to help interpret the spirit and outcomes of the Council. Pastors sought assistance with sacramental preparations at all levels, with Bible study, new liturgical orientations, and outreach programs for those in need.

What began in a small rural parish in Tiverton, Rhode Island, is illustrative of the generous response of RSCJ to service in the Church. It was a lovely omen that the name of the parish bore the name of the Society's founder, Saint Madeleine Sophie. In the year following the special chapter and shortly after cloister was lifted, several RSCJ of the community at Elmhurst, Convent of the Sacred Heart, in Portsmouth, Rhode Island, began helping with the Confraternity of Christian Doctrine (CCD), the religious education program on Saturday mornings at Saint Madeleine Sophie Parish, and staffing the parish office so the pastor, Father Hart, could have the afternoon off.

Joan Gannon, RSCJ, one of these volunteers, remembers that she found the words of the 1970 Chapter truly provocative, especially when they insisted that only prayerful communities located within (not apart from) the world would have the strength to take up the challenge of addressing the suffering and injustice that prevented so many from living full human lives. Sr. Gannon heard, in this Chapter document, a call to move out of the institution. Elmhurst had closed in 1972, and she was living at Stuart Country Day School in Princeton, New Jersey. For her, the logical place to go was back to Portsmouth to work in Saint Barnabas Parish, where the staff were eager to have sisters run the CCD and other programs. She contacted her good friend Lorette (Retsy) Piper, RSCJ, another adventurous soul, who was intrigued by this possibility. Eventually Sister Gannon met with the provincial team to explain her thinking: The RSCJ were a known entity in Portsmouth at Saint Barnabas Parish; they were wanted there; they had foundational parochial experience to build on; summer sessions at Boston College would provide more training.

The provincial team sent Sisters Piper and Gannon to Portsmouth to investigate the future possibility of the sisters working in parishes with the understanding that a third person would be added to the community. Phyllis Heuisler, RSCJ, at age 74, signed on. The three found a small apartment and set to work. According to Sister Gannon, "Retsy worked with the adults and I with the children: confirmation program, first communion program and other CCD classes. We visited the parishioners in their homes, developed strong and unifying programs, used our own theological convictions and recent training to bring quality to the education we offered, and learned immense amounts about 'real life.' It was a rich and liberating time for us." As with other new parish projects, the ministry grew exponentially as new needs presented themselves: ecumenical ventures, collaboration in prison ministry, services for people in poverty. Sister Gannon summed up her experience of their four years at Saint Barnabas: "I am convinced that that small step 'into the world' was, for me, the beginning of the life I was meant to live."

The chapter documents of 1967 and 1970 made new claims on the hearts of RSCJ. Some experienced the desire to explore new calls to meet specific needs. Individuals or small groups explored participation in parish work, often beginning with a period of volunteering. Parish experience led inevitably to much broader and varied work and frequently led to collaboration with religious of other orders.

The parish experience of the little group in Portsmouth was replicated across the province again and again, mostly by individual RSCJ rather than by groups. In the United States, Religious of the Sacred Heart have served in a wide variety of parish ministries. They have worked in large, well-established parishes and in underserved communities. They have teamed up with African Americans and Native Americans, with farm workers and with struggling and sometimes transient inner-city communities. Once cloister was lifted, the parish became the spiritual home for many of the religious. Noticing what was needed and offering to pick up some of the many tasks that keep a parish afloat seemed only natural.

That same generous instinct led, eventually, to RSCJ assuming parish leadership. The journey of Maureen Chicoine, RSCJ, is a case in point. After thirteen years as a member of the Parish Visitors of Mary Immaculate, Sister Chicoine transferred to the Society of the Sacred Heart in 1980. In 1985, her attraction to work in the local Church led her to become a parish faith formation director, and for the next ten years she developed and deepened the skills and experience to pastor a parish. She further prepared herself for leadership by taking a course on the administrative aspects of parish management and by culling the wisdom of women already engaged in such parish leadership roles.

In 1994, Sister Chicoine was appointed by Bishop Philip Straling of San Bernardino, California, to serve Saint Mary Magdalene parish in Corona, California, as "pastoral coordinator," a title allowed by canon law for non-ordained persons leading a parish. Bishop Straling encouraged her to take classes in preaching and lay presiding, and she preached regularly. Except for sacramental duties, she was the resident pastoral person, working with a deacon, a bookkeeper, and a religious education staff. She also participated with the clergy in diocesan meetings, including advising the bishop about personnel placements. During her tenure, the parish grew from 400 to 1,400 families.

In 2004, Bishop Gerald Barnes, Bishop Straling's successor, asked Sister Chicoine to merge three parishes, two predominantly Spanish-speaking, and the third having a large Vietnamese population. The name of this merged parish was Our Lady of Hope. The three parishes were not homogeneous, and a fair amount of distrust existed. The cultural differences were challenging, as were managing finances, dealing with debt, allocating limited meeting space, overseeing building plans, and, above all, meeting the needs of a young and growing population of about 4,000 families at two sites. There were multiple celebrations in three languages every weekend. An average month had thirty-six infant baptisms; an average year had several funerals. She coordinated first communions and initiations of new members at Easter. At one point among the staff of eighteen, Sister Chicoine was the only person who was neither Hispanic nor Vietnamese. One can only marvel at the challenges she faced during these eight years of pastoring at Our Lady of Hope.

Besides work at the parish level, several RSCJ accepted diocesan positions. In 1983, the *New Code of Canon Law* [55] allowed the possibility for a non-cleric to serve as diocesan chancellor. Mary B. Flaherty, RSCJ, became the first woman appointed to serve a major American diocese in that capacity when Archbishop John Quinn of San Francisco appointed her to that role. In 1994, she added the title and responsibilities of vicar for religious. Nancy Kane, RSCJ, was another to be appointed to a diocesan leadership role. She was named vicar for religious in the Diocese of San Diego in 1987, and added the title and work of academic dean of the diocesan St. Francis Seminary three years later.

Religious of the Sacred Heart have served the Church in a variety of other ways, including service on numerous boards, committees and councils. One opportunity to serve the Church worldwide was offered to Sister Hughes, who, in 1979 was invited as a guest to a meeting of the International Commission on English in the Liturgy (ICEL). ICEL was born during the third session of Vatican Council II when it became clear that some measure of vernacular prayer would be permitted in the revised liturgy. Every major language group assembled experts to provide vernacular translations of the Latin, as well as eventual revisions, adaptation, and original texts to serve the prayer of the Church. For nineteen years, Sister Hughes was a member of ICEL's advisory committee and eventually chaired the original text subcommittee, which provided, for example, about fifty original texts for the *Order of Christian Funerals* to supplement the bare bones offering of prayers in the Latin original. The advisory committee set policy and coordinated the work of scores of committees and hundreds of collaborators, trying to provide a language fitting to give God thanks and praise.

Shortly after completing an eleven-year revision of the Sacramentary in 1998, approved by every English-speaking conference of bishops, ICEL's work was derailed by new translation guidelines issued from Rome, requiring literal translations of the Latin rather than the language of dynamic equivalence.[56] Perhaps one day the 1998 translation will become a legitimate alternative translation for use across the English-speaking world. For now, it serves as a cautionary tale that service in the Church is not always a matter of unalloyed joy.

Conclusion

In considering these new ministries embraced by Religious of the Sacred Heart after the Second Vatican Council, two reflections come to mind.

The first reflection has to do with the criticism the Society of the Sacred Heart received for "abandoning the ministry" in the schools. The criticism generally included the implication that RSCJ were no longer being faithful to their vocation as envisioned by their founder, Madeleine Sophie Barat. And yet, Vatican II had encouraged religious to return to the original inspiration of the founder. Were RSCJ faithful to Sophie or were they deviating from her vision?

In the original *Constitutions* of 1815, Madeleine Sophie named four means for "glorifying the Sacred Heart of Jesus." In today's parlance, these means are providing formal education, working with the poor, offering retreats, and developing relationships with people outside of RSCJ communities.

In the United States, once public education was provided free of charge and the parochial school system expanded, there was no longer a need for the Society to conduct free schools as it had formerly done, so the Society gradually gave up operating parish schools. Before Vatican II, the Society's retreat work had been minimal, and collaboration with others had been limited by the rule of cloister. When people considered the work of the Society of the Sacred Heart, it was generally formal education in Sacred Heart schools that came to mind.

It would be fair to say that at the time of Vatican II the work of the Society in the United States was concentrated in the schools. Thus, recovery of other means of glorifying the Heart of Jesus was actually an act of fidelity to Sophie and her expansive vision of the Society's means of glorifying God. Seminary education is a form of formal education; houses of prayer, retreats, and spiritual direction are robust expressions of the *Constitutions'* call to offer retreats to persons living in the world; service in the Church, such as parochial ministry, is a rich form of collaboration with others.

A second reflection has to do with the way the ministries discussed above illustrate the concluding words of the post-baptismal anointing of the newly baptized, "so that, united with his people, you may remain forever a member of Christ who is Priest, Prophet and King."

These titles have long been applied to the role of the bishop as the one who sanctifies, teaches and rules the diocese he serves. But clearly these titles also name the clusters of ministries adopted by Religious of the Sacred Heart as women in the Church after the Second Vatican Council. Seminary education encompasses a *prophetic* role—teaching. Spiritual ministry, direction, and retreats name a *priestly* role—sanctifying. Parochial and other forms of Church leadership engage one in the role of *ruler*—leading others in the community of faith.

It seems important to claim what is true: namely, that the Society of the Sacred Heart continues to imitate the person and work of Christ, who, by his teaching, sanctifying and leading, invited all of us to share our gifts of mind and heart in imitation of his saving presence.

Ecumenical & Interfaith Ventures

For many Catholics, before the Second Vatican Council the term "Church" referred to the hierarchical institution, the repository of faith and sacred tradition. But following Vatican II, members of the Church began to be familiar with new names. Besides the Church as institution there was now the Church as Body of Christ, Church as sacrament, Church as herald, Church as servant.[57] The council documents also made clear that faith traditions other than Catholic, or even other than Christian, were part of God's plan and should be reverenced as such. These teachings opened Catholics to the more pastoral, Scripture-based call of Jesus in contrast to what had sometimes felt like Catholic triumphalism. Men and women religious, in their own prayer life and in their teaching, were inspired to open their tents to welcome people previously excluded.

Although the Religious of the Sacred Heart had been semi-cloistered from their inception, limitations on their physical movement had not imposed limitations on them mentally or spiritually. In the early 1960s, many communities of RSCJ had been privileged to attend or hear lectures by theologians from many faith traditions as they prepared for Vatican II. RSCJ were women of the Church, women who read the calls of Vatican II as an opening to embrace, as surely the Heart of Christ embraced, all persons of all faiths.

Katharine Hargrove, RSCJ, was without doubt a forerunner for some of this work, as she had been engaged in Jewish-Christian conversations from the early 1950s. A news release from the United States Province at the time of Sister Hargrove's death recounts how her mother had taught her "that Jesus was Jewish, and we must always respect the Jewish people and their religion." According to the release:

> From the 1960s until the 1990s, Sister Hargrove was active in the National Conference of Christians and Jews, serving for many years as that organization's program chairperson and national board member, and in the International Council of Christians and Jews. She was a member of the United States Bishops' Secretariat for Catholic-Jewish relations and worked with Vatican officials involved in interfaith relations.[58]

Rabbi James A. Rudin of New York, known for dedication to interreligious affairs, would say of her:

> She was in the first generation after the Second Vatican Council who really engaged the Jewish religion, Jewish religious leaders and the Jewish community in a way that had never been done before. I've always thought of her as one of the primary architects of the Vatican II encounter with Jews and Judaism, and she influenced a lot of other people. She belongs in the history books.[59]

Sister Hargrove recognized as a needed step the efforts following Vatican II to remove anti-Semitic language from textbooks and liturgical services. But she also wondered if the Church was going far enough. Was it really addressing the teachings and actions in the Church's history that had fostered anti-Semitism?

One of her four books, *Seeds of Reconciliation: Essays in Jewish-Christian Understanding,*[60] paired Christian and Jewish writers' dialogue under the following five sections: seeding, nourishing, winnowing, uprooting, and harvesting, clearly an attempt to show that Christian-Jewish dialogue was to be an area of new growth, with challenges to both groups to learn and appreciate each other. In the section on seeding, the authors address the conflicts between synagogue and Church. In the section on winnowing, the writers point out that the Holocaust raises for Jews the question of God's covenant with them and, at the same time, challenges Christians to examine the role of their negative theology of Judaism—specifically, the commonly held belief that the Jews killed Jesus— in contributing to that tragic historical outcome. (This belief was officially disavowed by the Catholic Church in 1965.) In his review of Sister Hargrove's book, T. Pawlikowski, OSM, states in conclusion, "This volume… actually sets the reader squarely in the middle of an ongoing conversation between leading figures in the twentieth-century Christian-Jewish encounter."[61]

Adele Fiske, RSCJ, also a professor at Manhattanville College, took another path in terms of exploring interfaith relations. Having for many years taught Greek and Roman studies, she began to focus on Eastern religions. In 1967, with support from a Fulbright grant, she set off for India to explore Hinduism and Indian Buddhism. She visited six major Buddhist centers in India. In her diaries she remarked that she had not gone as a scholar but as a pilgrim, for the peoples' experiences were important to her. She tried to learn the languages that would allow her to have face-to-face, rather than interpreted conversations, but that proved too difficult. The high point for her was the time she spent with the Dalai Lama. She wrote in her diary:

> He said he thinks of religions as being like branches of one government or different levels of instruction in one science, and that the great thing is for each religion to respect the other and even to learn from it. He repeated often his belief that the "root of the goal" of the great religions is the same, has to be the same. He emphasized the need for charity and for understanding. In Tibet, he said, everyone had to study Hinduism, but that Christianity was not known. Now Tibetan Buddhists want to learn about it

> and about its profound teaching. He said that it was really in its origin an Eastern religion and therefore should be easily at home here in spite of its Western development.[62]

Sister Fiske went on to remark that she and the Dalai Lama spoke of mysticism, of reincarnation versus Christian belief about the afterlife, of continuous creation, of nothingness and the individual.

Sister Fiske developed the Asian Studies program at Manhattanville so that not only she, but her students, could continue to delve into these concerns. Thomas Merton's writings and experiences with Eastern monasticism were also part of the milieu of that time.

Elizabeth Hoye, RSCJ, was another sister determined to promote interfaith exchanges. In the 1960s, she took her students at the Convent of the Sacred Heart on 91st Street in New York City to visit temples, synagogues and mosques. This approach had been inspired by the many talks and articles by theologians of many faith traditions in preparation for Vatican II. As this new openness to other religious traditions was explored, taught, and brought to prayer, she began to understand the line in John's Gospel, "In my Father's house there are many mansions." She felt called to set up a place where people could come together in shared belief of God's all-embracing love. For thirty years she, along with Mary Gen Smyth, RSCJ, operated Abba House, a House of Prayer, first at the Kenwood Convent, and later in another section of Albany. It was open to lay and religious, clergy, people of all faiths. According to Sister Hoye's Society obituary,[63] Abba House kept "a rhythm of daily prayer, in solitude and with others," and also engaged in study, prayer, and ecumenism. Sister Hoye participated in the Conference of Science and Faith of the Northeast Synod of the Presbyterian Church at Stony Point, New York, and co-sponsored a public ecumenical dialogue, "Experience of the Cross and Resurrection in the Work of Christian Unity."

As head of school at the Convent of the Sacred Heart in New York City, Joan Kirby, RSCJ, was aware of all the interfaith conversations taking place before, during, and after the close of Vatican II. After a period of working with homeless people in New York City, she would spend fourteen years at the Temple of Understanding, first as executive director, and then as its United Nations representative. The stated mission of the temple is to foster interfaith education and understanding. In 1975, the Temple of Understanding hosted the first interfaith conference to be held at the United Nations and laid the groundwork for its ongoing involvement. The work gave Sister Kirby a deep and broad experience of other religious faiths. When she was asked to become the executive director of the Temple of Understanding in 1994, she took on the challenge of teaching adult courses on interfaith dialogue, which "flourished and deepened during those years."[64] Sister Kirby wrote,

> People ask me why I practice Zen Buddhism. I do so because Buddhism has taught me to stop looking for Jesus "out there." For decades I sought to regenerate an inner awareness. I imitated the affections, feelings, attitudes of Jesus, but always as someone, something beyond me—outside—other than me. Buddhism has taught me to stop reaching, looking outside of my inner self.... I am Christ. I receive Christ as my food; I have been permeated by the living Jesus....This prompts me to live in the present moment because this is where God is.[65]

In 2010, the Temple of Understanding presented Sister Kirby with the Interfaith Visionary Lifetime Achievement Award for "promoting interreligious values at the United Nations, her lifelong commitment to addressing human rights and ecological issues, and her passionate devotion to the development of young leaders." United Nations Secretary General Ban Ki-Moon wrote at the time,

> We are especially mindful of the special role you have played in advancing the Millennium Development Goals[66] and interfaith and intercultural dialogue, as well as confronting climate change. I am also thankful that you have taken the time to nurture young global citizens from all parts of the world. Your leadership has been exemplary. Your influence profound. I thank you.

Institutional Responses

These women worked tirelessly to open themselves and those they worked with to the interconnectedness of all expressions of belief, but there were also institutional developments. Glen Oak School, founded in 1969, and Doane Stuart Academy, founded in a merger in 1975, were unique institutional expressions of the ecumenical and interfaith work of the Society.

Glen Oak, described in another chapter, was a new girls' school, located in a Cleveland suburb on property adjacent to Gilmour Academy, a Holy Cross Brothers' school for boys. It was, from its inception, open-spaced, interfaith, and inclusive of all races, religious traditions and economic situations. The board of trustees included ministers from different Christian denominations, as well as a rabbi, and the faculty likewise reflected the diversity of religious traditions.

Doane Stuart, on the other hand, represented the merger of two well-established schools, one the Roman Catholic Kenwood Academy (1852) and the other the Episcopal St. Agnes School (1870). The administrators of St. Agnes approached those at Kenwood because St. Agnes was slated to close and the Episcopalians did not want to lose their only school. The merger that occurred was unique. The new name of the school, Doane Stuart, honors Janet Erskine Stuart, RSCJ, an influential British educator, and the Right Reverend William Crosswell Doane, the first Episcopal Bishop of Albany. Janet Stuart was a former Anglican who adopted the Catholic faith and entered the Society. The Doane Stuart school began as ecumenical, but later became interfaith.

Both these institutions expanded the teaching of religion from focusing on one to exploring all. Vatican II had clearly mandated that all religious traditions were to be seen as paths for human beings to reach their full potential. For Catholics who might have been erroneously taught that one must be Catholic to be saved, there were updated teachings about salvation, church history, and the sacraments. Students began to study Scripture and to learn how to interpret it contextually rather than to accept it literally. They studied the history of divisions within Christianity, and learned how to affirm their own tradition without degrading those of others.

An Unfolding Future

Following Vatican II, every Catholic experienced change. The liturgy was now in the vernacular; the sacraments, which had always been the sole domain of the priest, now were opened to fuller participation by lay persons: eucharistic ministers, readers, eventually pastoral administrators. Teaching about the Church vis-a-vis other Christian denominations now asked for openness and dialogue. The proverbial window that had been opened by Vatican II understandably unsettled many who felt that some of what they had been taught or learned was now undermined or dismissed. It was a time of struggle in which Catholics needed re-education about the roots of their faith and its foundation in Judaism. The Religious of the Sacred Heart and the schools mentioned above, as well as the prayer groups affiliated with Abba House, undertook to bring new life to the Catholic tradition, while at the same time opening it out to greater understanding of other traditions. Sacred Heart schools around the country offered courses in world religions to ensure that upcoming generations of Catholics had a deeper grounding in their faith as it was being shaped by the teachings of Vatican II. Religious pluralism was to be seen as foundational to North America's values and, therefore, appreciated for what it offered.

Many years later, in a book titled *Seeking the One Whom they Love,*[67] Kathleen Hughes, RSCJ, and Therese F. Meyerhoff, then director of communications for the United States Province, would bring together reflections by Religious of the Sacred Heart on a wide variety of ways they prayed, adopting modes of prayer from other traditions, such as those of native peoples, Judaism, Buddhism, and Islam.

Like many other Catholics, RSCJ did not easily embrace the challenges, but they worked through them with persistence out of their desire to know more deeply the Heart of God and to reveal it to the world.

Educational Projects for the Underserved

Introduction

The calls of Vatican II and the Society's Special Chapter of 1967 stimulated Religious of the Sacred Heart to view the world and the ministry of education in new ways. Whether it was the documents coming out of Vatican II and the 1967 Special Chapter, or whether it was their own educational experiences that led them to hear new calls to ministries beyond the Society's institutions, it is clear that some of the RSCJ in each province began to move out of the congregation's schools into new settings. In the closing remarks of the chapter, they had been reminded by the superior general of Madeleine Sophie Barat's admonition to always seek the means to strengthen and make more authentic the Society's treasured *Cor Unum*, the union of minds and hearts.

As noted in a previous chapter, there were inevitably differences of opinion among the religious about what they were being called to do in these times. There were those who felt strongly that the focus should be on what the religious could do through the Society's schools and those who felt equally strongly that education meant far more than what happens in classrooms. The Society's *Cor Unum* motto was tested time and time again. Nevertheless, the religious began to move outward. This chapter will describe several projects that pushed the mission of education into new venues and new forms, taking it to communities not generally represented by the traditional Sacred Heart schools. Individual RSCJ found ways to bring marginalized groups into Sacred Heart institutions and to carry the mission outward to the underserved.

Broadening the Traditional View of Education

Some of the initial impetus for expansion came from RSCJ involved with colleges, perhaps because they had wider access to information and experiences. For example, as early as the 1950s, years before Vatican II, Patricia Barrett, RSCJ, professor at the Society's Maryville College in St. Louis, became concerned after reading about conflicts between police and impoverished members of the community. Seeking a way to help both sides, she set up a night course at Maryville so that officers could learn new ways of interacting more effectively.

Another example came from San Francisco, where RSCJ Constance Welch and Gertrude Patch at the Society's Lone Mountain College felt that the college, and education generally, could benefit from greater diversity. They also recognized that students from marginalized communities often did not have access to education that would prepare them for college. In the 1970s, they set up the Hunter's Point degree program at Lone Mountain, allowing many African-American students to work toward and receive a college degree and often to go into teaching.

Patricia Schaffer, RSCJ, a professor of science at San Diego College for Women (now part of University of San Diego) took another route. She too realized the need for outreach if education was to truly respond to the call of the Church to meet the needs of the world. In 1978 she set up the organization known as the Founder's Club as a way of engaging students in continuing the Society's educational mission. Founder's Club members responded to the social needs of the broader San Diego community and traveled to Mexico to build houses and offer tutoring. This club remains very much alive at USD.

Moving Beyond the Society's Schools

Each of the RSCJ discussed so far found ways to use the resources of Sacred Heart institutions to enrich the lives of the underserved, while other RSCJ would eventually make more definitive breaks from Society owned and operated institutions, although in most cases this happened gradually.

In Omaha, Rosemary Moody, RSCJ, who held degrees in counseling and psychology, returned from making her final profession in Rome where, in the Society's tradition, each group of newly professed RSCJ, received a name and a motto. Her group had been designated *La Vrai Vie,* "the real life." Sister Moody had taught at Barat College in Lake Forest, Illinois, and Duchesne College in Omaha, Nebraska, but after her final profession, she lived out her group's motto by working with disadvantaged youth in Omaha to foster their educational growth. She did this by first working with the Job Corps, a federal government program for helping young people gain work skills and find employment. She also served as a probation officer of the juvenile court. Eventually, she incorporated many Job Corps courses into a community college curriculum. These courses were a good fit because they were useful, flexible, financially reasonable, and they led to self-development and employment.

Next, Sister Moody turned to working with preschoolers as director of Head Start in Omaha, the federal program to promote school readiness, and then to overseeing thirty-five Head Start programs in Chicago. Returning to Lake Forest in 1974, she worked with the federally funded Upward Bound, an educational program for high school students. She also joined with others who had set up a program to support single mothers continuing their education. Barat College offered special help, on-campus housing, and child care. Next, Sister Moody worked in the Lake County community college system to improve the general education of young people, veterans, and returning students, and to help them develop their skills for employment.

In all these endeavors, Sister Moody was expressing the deeper meaning of *La Vrai Vie* by recognizing others' realities and, with support from Sacred Heart institutions and governmental programs, helping them expand their opportunities. Her obituary celebrated her as one who could be called on for anything, no matter how difficult the task. At one time, she helped rescue a student who had left home and become involved with the motorcycle gang known as Hell's Angels. Sister Moody went in search of the girl, entered the house where she was living, talked to the group, and convinced the girl to come home with her.

In 1968, Carol Putnam, RSCJ, a professor of art and philosophy at Newton College of the Sacred Heart, was asked to join the urban task force of the Archdiocese of Boston. This experience made such an impression on her that she later said it had determined her future work. Cardinal Cushing funded this task force, an inter-congregational religious collaboration to bring positive change to the Catholic parochial schools in the Roxbury-South End neighborhoods of Boston. Sister Putnam continued to teach one class at Newton Colleege, and because she wanted to involve her students in the new work, she brought student volunteers into the project.

Eventually, the archdiocesan urban task force disbanded, but this first experience of working closely with the poor and victims of discrimination set Sister Putnam on the trail she would blaze from Boston to Florida and California, to the advantage of refugees and migrant workers.

Sister Putnam's next project in Boston would be a social service center for Hispanics, known as Casa del Sol. In a report on her ministries, she wrote:

> I moved on to help develop a program for Hispanic women, mostly Puerto Ricans, who were locked into cold tenements not knowing the [English] language nor having saleable skills. We started Casa del Sol for them. Their first request was for English classes, and then for helping them get jobs. We ended up providing classes in typing, bookkeeping, preparation for GED diploma, etc., not only for Hispanic women, but for their men and for the street kids in the area.

The genesis of another effort, a mission in Indiantown, Florida, came about after Sister Putnam and Joan Gannon, RSCJ, spent a year of exploration and discernment together. At the end of that time, the provincial team of the Boston-based Washington Province happily endorsed their decision to set up a ministry in Indiantown, in the Diocese of West Palm Beach, Florida. The sisters would work with an underserved population in the Miami region, where the Carrollton School of the Sacred Heart was located. Constance Dryden, RSCJ, waiting for the provincial of East Africa to allow her to begin work in Kenya, joined them for a year. The pastor of Holy Cross Catholic Church in Indiantown, Father Frank O'Loughlin, felt the greatest need was for a day care program for migrant children, and Sister Putnam set to work developing that. Working with the parish and townspeople, the sisters helped to create a new neighborhood, including housing and gathering spaces, principally for the migrant community. They set up a variety of services, taught religious education and worked in the clinic. The pastor then suggested beginning a school for the children. Thus began Hope Rural School in 1980, a full-time school dedicated to the needs of migrant children. Again, in Sister Putnam's words:

> The pupils are Mexican, Puerto Rican, Cuban, Haitian, Mayan-Indian, and American Black and White. Not all are from farmworker families. The focus is on three things: providing the kind of permanence missing from migrant life, respect for the culture of each child, and strong development of the three R's. The children were hungry to learn. One little Mexican boy was heard to say excitedly to his friend: "Let's stay in from recess so we can get smarter quicker!"

Sister Gannon wrote in an email about those years,

> We were immersed in the multicultural (Anglo, Mexican, Haitian, Guatemalan, Puerto Rican, African American) town community, and we did whatever needed to be done. Those eight years were probably the most complex and richest in my life, and I tend to see it all in technicolor.

On the other coast, in El Cajon, California, the parents of developmentally disabled preschoolers rejoiced when Religious of the Sacred Heart agreed to set up an educational program for their children. Mary (Be) Mardel, RSCJ, remembered:

> We had a Saturday religion class for eight or ten children who were physically or mentally handicapped. Young RSCJ and novices worked with them, prepared them for first communion, and loved them. Because at that time, California did not provide support for such children until first grade, the parents begged us to help them during the week.

With a gift of $25,000 from a generous friend, the sisters were able to provide a tiny two-room building on land adjoining the site of the former Convent of the Sacred Heart in El Cajon. In 1966, Sara (Sally) Rude, RSCJ, who had a master's degree in special education, took charge of what came to be called St. Madeleine Sophie's School for Exceptional Children. She was succeeded in 1968 by Maxine Kraemer, RSCJ, who became a driving force as a fundraiser, construction overseer, bus driver, and civic advocate for the education of exceptional children.

In 1972, the Society closed the Sacred Heart school in El Cajon, California, and in 1975, a new federal law required public schools to educate with special services all school-age students with disabilities. Sister Kraemer saw, though, that for the developmentally disabled, formal education should not end with high school, and the program for developmentally disabled children was redesigned as a center to serve developmentally disabled adults. Later, Sister Kraemer earned local and national recognition for her successful efforts to integrate adults at the center into community jobs. St. Madeleine Sophie's Center continues today with a staff of 110 and a budget of over $4 million, funded mostly by the state.

In Houston, Lillian Conaghan and Elizabeth (Betsy) Hartson, both RSCJ, took the Society's educational mission to Our Lady of Guadalupe, a parish-operated "barrio school" that served a marginalized Hispanic community. The sisters began as volunteers at the parish, teaching religion part-time in the school, as there was no money for religious education. Then Paula Toner, RSCJ, began to divide her time between Duchesne Academy in Houston and the parish school, thus beginning a partnership incorporating the Sacred Heart Fathers who staffed the parish, the archdiocese, and the Religious of the Sacred Heart. This partnership expanded into all areas of the parish life and drew RSCJ from other parts of the country.

In 1982, after the five United States provinces merged into a single province, Clare Pratt, RSCJ, who had been the provincial of the Boston-based Washington Province, moved to Houston to become the administrator at the school; and Rose Marie Quilter, RSCJ, moved from the former New York Province to become director of religious education. Emma Fernandez, RSCJ and Elia (Tootsie) Torian, both RSCJ from the St. Louis Province, worked with the youngest students and took over religious education in the upper school. Eventually, Grail McMullen, RSCJ, became the parish secretary; Laura Anderson, RSCJ, taught math; and Ana Vila, RSCJ from Puerto Rico, served as librarian, provided counseling and convened women's groups. Parents and alumnae from Duchesne Academy became involved, drawing the entire Sacred Heart family into a different part of Houston, almost another world, while pulling the people from both worlds toward the center of the Heart.

In Canada, in 1979, when the Convent of the Sacred Heart, Point Grey, British Columbia, closed, it became an opening for the RSCJ to respond to the need for women religious to provide services in northern Canada. Sisters Mary Elizabeth (Sally) McLean, Pamela Yell, and Anne-Marie Conn, then a second-year novice, headed north to the Yukon Territory, where the bishop was looking for teachers for the Catholic schools. Whitehorse, the capital of the Yukon, is situated among the coastal and Rocky Mountains along the Yukon River; and among its residents are indigenous First Nations peoples. As a community, the sisters were involved in a variety of ways in the parish in the area. It was a new kind of ministry, non-urban, and non-institutional, and the religious worked in collaboration with all around them.

"Beautiful and untamed," Sister Conn described the area in a report on the sisters' work there. Sister Yell was named religious education assistant at Sacred Heart parish, Sister McLean went to work at the junior high school, and Sister Conn taught in the elementary school. At the same time, there was a residence in

Whitehorse called Yukon Hall, where the First Nations children lived and which was run by First Nations women. The children who lived there were mostly from the outlying communities and from home situations that were not safe. "Often on a Friday evening, we would have a number of children from Yukon Hall land on our doorstep, as they had nowhere to go; yet as teens, they could be out until 9:30 or 10 p.m."

In the second year of the mission, Ann McManus, RSCJ, joined the group. The sisters' house not only served the parish and the youth, but often welcomed women religious serving in outlying small communities. "In our minds this move came about to meet the expressed needs in our country," Sister Conn said. But over the next several years "in the minds of those in leadership in the province," the area, though underserved, was deemed "too far away" from other RSCJ, so in 1986 the sisters left Whitehorse.

There remained among some in the province a longing to continue ministering to the people of northern Canada, so the sisters opened a house to serve the needs in Prince George, a city in northern British Columbia. It continues to this day, with Sisters McLean and Mary Ann Bates, who had replaced Sister Conn at Whitehorse.

Challenges and Gleanings from These Works

The religious who founded Casa del Sol in Boston, the ministry at Indiantown, the center for exceptional adults at El Cajon, and those who lived the mission at Whitehorse and Our Lady of Guadalupe were responding to calls from the local Church, the Society, and the world. They experienced worlds that often were not far from where they lived; and yet, when they crossed into these unfamiliar neighborhoods, they found profound differences. Once the sisters experienced the needs of these neighbors, they became committed to finding ever new ways to respond.

The sisters understood themselves as educators who learned from their students even as they provided instruction. They understood that they needed to allow the people to whom they ministered to become their teachers. Recognition of the needs challenged them, in view of their vow of education, to adopt ministries beyond the scope of the Society's classrooms and schools. Content, while still important, became secondary to understanding each person's needs. Traditional content often had to be rethought and adapted to the contexts of the people before them. Paulo Freire strongly influenced these efforts at adaptation. He wrote in his 1968 classic, *Pedagogy of the Oppressed*: "No pedagogy which is truly liberating can remain distant from the oppressed by treating them as unfortunates and by presuming, for their emulation, models from among the oppressors. The oppressed must be their own example in the struggle for redemption."[68]

A Different Path: Setting Up a School

At the same time, in New York City, Ruth Dowd, RSCJ, philosophy professor at Manhattanville College of the Sacred Heart in Purchase, New York, became involved in weekend tutoring at All Saints Catholic School in Harlem. Nancy McMahon, who worked with her, wrote, "It was 1967-68 when she initiated planning for Harlem Prep . . . in response, I am sure, to the Church's and the Society's call for "a preference for the poor." I don't think she thought of herself being "called," but just that "of course we should do this!"

Sister Dowd became acclimated to this population and its particular needs. She explored spaces for a new type of school, sought funding and networked with community organizers and educators. She worked with Dr. Eugene Callender, head of the New York Urban League, and formed a working relationship with Ed Carpenter, an African-American man who had taught in the New York City schools. Together they found a run-down grocery store at Eighth Avenue and 136th Street, in a neighborhood where there was little to engage young people, and with the monies raised, they leased the property and turned it into a school.

In the book *A Way Out of No Way: Harlem Prep: Transforming Dropouts into Scholars, 1967*-1977,[69] authors Hussein Ahdieh and Hillary Chapman write about "several sisters, including Dowd, Elizabeth McLoughlin, Oonah Ryan, and Jane Early, who became core members of this project," expressing their admiration for their dedication:

> The sisters from Manhattanville College served the students of Harlem Prep selflessly, playing a vital role in helping to make the school a reality. . . . Sisters Dowd, McLoughlin, and Early shared an apartment in the neighborhood—a huge change for them from the safe predictability of cloistered living. They also made the transition from full habits to civilian clothes. Together, the three sisters drove their Dodge Dart to school each morning. Fired by the social mission of the Gospels, they were totally dedicated to their service. When other employees arrived early at 7:30, the sisters were already there. When the last employee left at 4:30, they stayed to continue their work. They often offered their salaries back to the school. In fact, once one of the sisters threw the money upward, saying, "Jesus keep what you want in the air and let the rest fall to the ground."

Sister Dowd engaged Manhattanville College, the New York Board of Regents, the Urban League, and others to get the school accredited. The religious worked diligently with the students not only to improve the skills needed for graduation, but to inculcate in them the dream of further education. The sisters even suggested particular colleges, helping students visit and complete the application forms. Sister Dowd could "speak college," having been at Manhattanville for so many years, and she could bridge the cultural gap between the students and admissions officers. She was relentless in ensuring that students got good financial support, and she saw to it that the religious kept in touch with the students after they went off to school. Nancy McMahon recalled overhearing a student who returned from a rural college in upstate New York say, "Mother Dowd, more happens in Harlem in a snow blizzard on a Tuesday night at 3 a.m. than *ever* happened in this college!" She encouraged him to stick it out, although she agreed with him.

Sister Ryan, who had been in the initial group that went to Harlem, was replaced by Sister McLoughlin, in the second year. In reality, it appeared that the students and parents saw the sisters as somewhat interchangeable. They were curious as to why these women didn't have children, but instead had left their families and come to Harlem. As the authors of *A Way Out of No Way* wrote:

> Sister Liz met with the mother of one Harlem Prep student and anticipated discussing the student. Instead . . . the mother wanted to talk about her marriage, even though Sister Liz was single and only twenty-seven. The religious understood why staff and students might not be clear about their life choices, but that did not stand in the way of their recognizing this place as a vital expression of their educational mission, or of the students and staff's recognizing them as "family."

In 1972, Sister Dowd received the Woman of Conscience award from the National Council of Catholic Women for her work in responding to the educational needs in Harlem.

In 1977, ten years after Harlem Prep began, it was no longer possible to get funding to sustain it as an independent school, and it became part of the New York City public school system. However, the short lifespan of this project does not dim the experience gained and the lives changed.

Donald T. Streets, in a review of *A Way Out of No Way* for the *Journal of Bahá'í Studies*,[70] captures the spirit of the school. It created "a social context that that I might label a 'culture of inclusion'—one in which everyone who is a part of the school community matters, is respected, is related to in an authentic way, and is truly loved."

Reflections on the People and Projects

Throughout these years, because of the teachings of Vatican II and the Society's chapter calls, RSCJ, individually and in groups, were drawn to take the Society's mission beyond its schools to marginalized communities. At first, individual RSCJ found ways to bring people from marginalized groups into the Society's institutions, or partnered with others in order to broaden the Society's contacts with marginalized people. Later, RSCJ set up stand-alone projects or schools that expressed expanding understandings of the educational mission.

The impact of these choices was deeply felt by the RSCJ and the alumnae. As RSCJ moved out of cloistered communities, and as habits were left behind by sisters who wanted to lessen the distance with the world around them, the varying choices were often confusing and even conflictual. These tensions were exacerbated by the closing of some Sacred Heart schools, even as RSCJ moved into new, nontraditional schools. While the challenges of moving out into marginalized communities were exhilarating for many, the changes created feelings of sadness, loss, and even anger in others. As the Spirit blew open the traditional way of understanding the Society's educational mission, all were called to remember and recognize the wisdom in the words of the Society's founder, Madeleine Sophie Barat: "The times change, and we too must modify and change."[71]

New Initiatives Within Sacred Heart Schools

From the early days of the Society of the Sacred Heart, social justice was at the heart of Sacred Heart education. This is clear from Madeleine Sophie Barat's insistence that for every academy founded for children of upper-class families, there was to be a school for children of working class families who needed a different type of education. Although this requirement was nullified in the United States with the onset of public education and the parochial school system, the concern for social justice not only remained, but it was amplified in the years following Vatican II and inspired changes within Sacred Heart schools. The council's message that social justice was integral to life as a Catholic Christian came to be more clearly articulated in both the curriculum and the activities of the Sacred Heart schools. Each school explored the world around itself, internationally and locally, seeking ways to respond to perceived needs. Sometimes the responses led to specific projects, while at other times they led to deeper institutional change. This chapter will highlight some of the ways the schools brought the calls of Vatican II to life.

Justice-related Programs

In the 1960s, Annette Zipple, RSCJ, an administrator at the Academy of the Sacred Heart in Grosse Pointe, Michigan, developed the Sacred Heart Enrichment Program (SHEP), a thematic arts program for middle school girls that as of 2020 was still providing enrichment through the arts in southwest Detroit. This project broke the boundaries of economics and race, not by addressing it with discussion, but through creative and shared experiences that formed relationships. While this was not an official program of the academy, it brought central city children to the academy, where they engaged directly with students at the school, fostering face- to-face exchanges and learning. Later, Sister Zipple, along with members of other religious congregations, would found Our Lady of Guadalupe School for middle school girls as a way to continue this work of faith in action.

Suzanne Rogers, RSCJ, teaching high school at the Academy of the Sacred Heart in Buffalo, New York, was struck by the numbers of students who, though their families might have taken them on trips to Europe, were much less well acquainted with their own United States. She decided to build a month-long experiential trip for students to learn about their own country, with a focus on issues different from those in the cities where they were living. The students and teachers rented a van, committed to eating peanut butter and jelly sandwiches for daily lunches (how better to learn how so many survive day to day?), and to reading history and literature related to the places they would be visiting. Each night at dinner, they reflected together on what they had learned. As the group traveled westward, the students learned about the impact of geography on the population, about the role of rivers in the development of communities, and about the United States' government's displacement of Native Americans. The students met with people in small towns and on reservations, learning firsthand what textbooks only touched on. The evening reflections helped them begin to connect texts with people and experiences, sometimes raising doubts about the veracity of the texts. Students returned home with deeper knowledge of their country and primed to question and to seek first-hand evidence from all sides in their search for truth.

Nancy Bremner, RSCJ, was the assistant superior in charge of the work of the coadjutrix sisters at Barat College and then at Woodlands Academy of the Sacred Heart, both in Lake Forest, Illinois. In her role, she worked with the sisters who had often immigrated from other countries, did not have a college education, and did the domestic work in the Society's large institutions. She acquired certification in teaching English as a Second Language (ESL) as a way of helping both the coadjutrix sisters and the student boarders from Latin America, who often struggled with their school work. As Sister Bremner reflected on Scripture and prayed with the sisters, she felt called to reach out to those unnoticed and sometimes shunned communities that were, as she put it, "just around the corners of our lives."

Once cloister was lifted for the nuns, Sister Bremner took students to nearby urban areas, such as downtown Chicago and the Cabrini Green housing development on the city's Near North Side, enabling students to benefit from experiencing areas that were seemingly so close one could almost touch them, yet so far they were all but invisible. The students collected clothing, books, food, and art supplies, and took them to the Cabrini Green project. At the nearby Saint Joseph Church and School, academy students engaged in educational projects with the children while learning more about life just down the highway.

Sister Bremner also made contact with several Catholic schools in North Chicago and Waukegan, Illinois, and every year invited three or four classes to Woodlands for a safe, fun Halloween. Every high school class at Woodlands played a role. Some were greeters and treaters. Others helped with carving pumpkins, making masks and costumes, and building a spook house. One year, this annual project led to an important lesson in cultural differences. The class managed to obtain a large refrigerator box and decided to turn it into a fake coffin. When the groups of children exited the spook house on Halloween, the top of the coffin would rise as the volunteer lying inside sat up and peered out. On this occasion, three fourth-grade boys were so freaked out by the coffin that they ran off. Then, a short time later, they sneaked back to go through the spook house a second time, this time kicking the sides of the coffin and frightening the student lying inside.

Afterwards, during the Woodlands students' reflection time, when some complaints surfaced about the boys' behavior, their teacher asked them to think about what would happen to boys who became frightened in their more privileged neighborhoods. The students began to recognize how fear in some cultures could be interpreted as weakness and might leave boys who showed fear open to being bullied or hurt. Perhaps in the Halloween incident, the boys felt they had to return and kick the coffin to show they were not afraid.

For the academy students, experience with and reflection on life in communities that were so close yet so different shed a new light on the gospel message. Further, Sister Bremner's open embrace of the people they met made these programs very attractive to students.

A very different kind of program was instituted in Lake Forest in response to Vatican II's call not only to action, but to growth in the spirituality that was its life source. To that end, Helen Condon, RSCJ, head of school at Woodlands Academy of the Sacred Heart, Lake Forest, teamed with Richard Westley, a theology professor at Barat College, to offer some weekend workshops in Sacred Heart spirituality. In the beginning, the workshops were offered to sophomores and juniors in the schools of the Chicago Province and later were opened to students from outside the province. The workshops offered both challenges and fun, mainstays of adolescent development. It was an opportunity for the students to learn the history of Sacred Heart spirituality, to reflect on how that spirituality was expressed in Sacred Heart schools and in relationships with others, and to learn to pray with a heart of love. As one measure of the program's success, ten students were set on the path to religious life. On a broader level, it is interesting to note that the program was an early example of direct collaboration between lay and religious.

Newton Academy of the Sacred Heart in Newton, Massachusetts, began a program called *Hesed*, a Hebrew word meaning love. Students who participated went from the Boston suburbs into Roxbury and other low-income locales, where they worked with students from the neighborhood, delivered needed goods, arranged for shared events, and then returned to Newton for reflection.

Stone Ridge School of the Sacred Heart in Bethesda, Maryland, at the initiative of Margaret Brown, RSCJ, and Barbara Rogers, RSCJ, set in motion a symposium on the United States bishops' pastoral letter on war and peace, "The Challenge of Peace: God's Promise and Our Response" (1983). Students in Sacred Heart schools across the country were invited to read the pastoral, meet with church and civic leaders in their locality, specifically their bishop, and discuss how the pastoral was being enacted. They explored the document and implementation plans from the perspectives of church and political leaders and were encouraged to ask the leaders how they planned to promote the document's message. Each school was then invited to send two students and a faculty member to the symposium, which featured a panel of prominent leaders moderated by journalist Ted Koppel. Sacred Heart peace activist Anne Montgomery, RSCJ, was among panel members who explored ways to continue the work set forth in the pastoral letter.

Again, the academies were not only sowing the seeds of action on behalf of justice, but embodying it in educational experiences.

As early as 1968, Carrollton School of the Sacred Heart in Miami, Florida, began a relationship with the Barnyard project, sponsored by the organization Coconut Grove Cares. Georgie Blaeser, RSCJ, connected the school and the after-school project, In 1994, Rosemary Bearss, RSCJ, became the financial director for the sponsoring group and also became involved with programs and fundraising, connecting the students from Carrollton and the Barnyard.

Several schools responded to a call for help from Religious of the Sacred Heart who were founding a Sacred Heart school in Taipei, Taiwan. Students were invited to contribute money to buy bricks for the school building. In the process, students learned about the split of Taiwan from mainland China and how the RSCJ had been forced to flee the mainland. Since then, schools of the Network of Sacred Heart Schools have raised money to build schools in Uganda and Haiti, meeting sisters from those places and enlarging their sense of the open Heart of Christ.

When Mary Catherine McKay, RSCJ, went to Nicaragua, Lynne Lieux, RSCJ, who had been a novice under Sister McKay's direction, became keenly interested in the plight of the people of that country. When the opportunity presented itself, Sister Lieux began to take students there to do service work. For thirteen years students and faculty from the schools in New Orleans and Grand Coteau, Louisiana, and from Houston, Texas, participated in faculty-student groups working with Amigos for Christ in Nicaragua. They dug ditches, laid pipes for water to be brought into local communities, built schools and playgrounds, provided smoke-free ovens and improved sanitation in various ways. Students, faculty and local community members worked side by side and did not let language differences get in the way.

Service-learning experiences such as these eventually became a central element of programming offered by the Network of Sacred Heart Schools.

A new school experiment builds on a sister's vision

Helen Sheahan, RSCJ, provincial of the Society's Chicago Province, was approached by alumnae who wanted a Sacred Heart school in Cleveland, Ohio.

Their request came in the late 1960s, around the time that other Sacred Heart schools were closing. Duchesne College in Omaha, Nebraska, announced that it was closing in 1968 after sixty years of operation. In the New York Province, the Academy of the Sacred Heart in Rochester was closing after 113 years because of low enrollment. Clearly, opening a new school would be a great risk, especially since Cleveland already had several all-girls schools with fine histories. At this time, Isabel Cogan, RSCJ, was studying at the University of Chicago, writing her master's thesis on a new educational model based on the research of John Goodlad.[72] As the alumnae persisted, Sister Sheahan offered them the possibility of a different type of Sacred Heart school, one based on Sister Cogan's vision.

The result was Glen Oak School in Gates Mills, Ohio, and the type of education it represented was everything John Goodlad could have asked for. In *Education News* for September, 1968, he wrote:

> The educational reform movement of the past decade has been productive of ideas; it has not been so productive of educational change. We need to put into effect… a whole range of educational changes from building design to school organization to classroom instruction and to pupil learning. This is as true of the suburban environment as it is for the ghetto.[73]

In her master's thesis, Sister Cogan imagined a space that would be ecumenical, open-spaced, and racially and economically mixed. "Perhaps the most fundamental change envisioned is its affective-orientation," she wrote. "This will indeed affect the building design, organizational structure, the student-teacher relationship, and the methods of learning …."

The curriculum would include home economics, typing and computer skills, and experiential education. While the alumnae clearly wanted the new school modeled after the traditional Sacred Heart schools they had known and loved, they cast their lot, money, and hopes with the RSCJ as educators. And thus Glen Oak School was begun.

The sisters purchased land on property owned by Gilmour Academy, an all-boys' school run by the Brothers of the Holy Cross. They hired an architect with a mandate to develop a building with a large open space and a resource area at the center, intended to allow for all sorts of learning configurations. Sister Cogan was to be the principal, and Sister Sheahan asked the provincials of the four other provinces to support this new venture by making it inter-provincial. To that end, she sent a letter to all the RSCJ, inviting anyone who was interested in teaching in this new school to send her resume and reasons for wanting to be involved. This approach of asking RSCJ to volunteer to work in a project outside their own provinces was new. Sisters came from the Washington, San Francisco, and Chicago provinces. The motherhouse in Rome even sent an RSCJ from another country.

Unlike Harlem Prep, which is described in the chapter on educational projects for the underserved, Glen Oak was in a well-to-do suburb and featured a rigorous education in the usual disciplines. But it drew from a vast number of intersections and experiences. The goal was to enable the "people of God" to learn from one another and build a unity that crossed boundaries among institutional religions and bridged local Cleveland divisions.

Glen Oak board members included a rabbi, a Protestant minister, and members drawn from the various localities represented in the student population. Instead of the usual method of measuring student progress with grades, Glen Oak chose evaluations done by students and teachers, contending that comments aimed at enhancing skill development would allow the students to grow from their individual starting points.

As Sister Cogan wrote in her master's thesis, "The basic concept underlying the curriculum is that the uniqueness of each student must be fostered in order to give effective testimony to the dignity of the person." The academic disciplines were not seen as distinct but rather as intersecting entities. Again, the goal was to understand that learning affects every aspect of life. Teachers worked as teams, giving students room to develop independent projects that wove together various aspects of their learning.

Sister Cogan continued, "Human development thrives only in authentic interpersonal relationships. Broad representation of ethnic, racial, religious and socio-economic groups facilitates attaining this objective in a setting which enables the student to exercise leadership and to serve other persons in a pluralistic society." Her point was that everyone was there to learn from the others.

Glen Oak showed its flexibility and responsiveness when it began to share teachers and classes with Gilmour Academy, the adjacent all-male Holy Cross Brothers' school. There was friction when some Gilmour teachers tried to give grades, while the girls wanted more informative evaluations. However, some Gilmour teachers did embrace the new flexibility. These exchanges pushed each school to renew itself, to become more grounded in the students' present-day needs. Eventually, humor and persistence brought about greater adaptability from Gilmour's faculty and broader possibilities for both schools. After ten years, Glen Oak was taken over by Gilmour Academy, ending the educational experiment in its initial form. But to the credit of its vision and experience, in September 2019, Glen Oak alumnae held their fiftieth reunion and almost 200 women returned.

The Network is Formed

As one of its provisions, Vatican II mandated that religious communities adapt their lifestyles to enable them to meet the needs of the contemporary world. Religious orders that identified themselves as both contemplative and apostolic were required to clarify their status. For the Society of the Sacred Heart, which had been founded as an apostolic congregation, this meant giving up cloister in order to be able to establish closer relationships with students and their families. At the same time, other changes were set in motion. Until 1967, the Society had been organized into vicariates closely dependent on the central authority, the superior general and her council. After the Society's Special Chapter 1967, the vicariates were reconstituted as provinces—five in the United States, each composed of communities of sisters and schools from several states. RSCJ were assigned by their provincial superiors to work in the Sacred Heart schools situated within their province. If a school needed more funding or more sisters, this need was addressed by the provincial. Around this time, vocations to religious life began to decrease and soon there were not enough sisters to manage the schools. The schools were reconstituted as independent corporations often governed by predominantly lay boards with some RSCJ membership.

By 1970, ideas had been circulating about how the schools in the five United States provinces might work towards some unifying structure. One idea was given shape by Catherine (Kit) Collins, RSCJ. While each school would continue to be governed by its own board, the schools, under Sister Collins's leadership, became members of a Network of Sacred Heart Schools. What tied them together was a common educational philosophy rooted in the Society's mission of making known the love of the Heart of Christ, while allowing for considerable diversity in the way each school embodied the mission. By 1975, after a long process involving school administrators, faculties, students, parents and the religious, the network adopted five goals, with criteria under each, for carrying out the mission. These goals are a clear response to the calls of Vatican II, which insist that a Catholic must develop not only a personal faith in God, but one that impels to action on behalf of justice. The goals call for:

- A personal and active faith in God
- A deep respect for intellectual values
- A social awareness which impels to action
- The building of community as a Christian value
- Personal growth in an atmosphere of wise freedom

Although the five goals remain constant because they clearly express the essence of Sacred Heart education, the criteria are revised periodically to reflect the needs of the times.

Impact of Changes

Clearly, many RSCJ were drawn to the alternative expressions of the Society's charism described in this book and rejoiced in new freedoms that allowed them to be out among people from various walks of life. At the same time, despite the best intentions of those who were trying to adapt the Society's educational mission to the calls of Vatican II, there were skeptics among the RSCJ and alumnae who felt the Society was being drawn away from, or even abandoning, its essential mission. It was a time when some felt the phrase "educational mission" was being stretched to fit every kind of project a person or group espoused. Many were saddened or even angered, wondering why change was even necessary. The end of cloister, the changes in dress worn by the religious, the diversification of works, and maybe just the changing times led some to leave the congregation altogether. It was often hard for people with differing views to listen to one another with love.

Joan Magnetti, RSCJ, writing for this publication, reflected on the feelings and questions engendered by these times as RSCJ sought ways to follow the calls of the Church and the world:

> I experienced the tail end of a cloistered life, with its almost five hours of daily prayer, rules of silence and never leaving the grounds except for medical or educational reasons. My novice mistress allowed me to post the *New York Times* news on the bulletin board when the paper was on strike so we could at least pray for the world, if not live in it. She sent us, a little band of white veiled novices, to work with Father Howard Hubbard (later to become Bishop of Albany) in his storefront in Albany, where I had my first experience of children in the cold of winter who didn't have socks.
>
> Later, I taught and administered in Network schools and spent summers in Harlem helping groups that were directly engaged with low-income children. Often Network children and alumnae joined in these endeavors. After final vows, I spent a short time in Upper Egypt working with Beatrice Brennan, RSCJ, in poor Arab villages, where half the children died of dysentery by the age of five, and many became blind from flies carrying disease from camel dung. It broke my heart. I sat on a rooftop in the village watching little girls pick the bugs off of cotton bolls hour after hour. No schooling, no future. I resolved if I ever administered a Sacred Heart school, I would never forget those little girls, nor would the girls under my tutelage be able to forget them.
>
> Over the next thirty-two years, I was headmistress of the Sacred Heart schools in Princeton, New Jersey, and Greenwich, Connecticut. Those schools, along with other Sacred Heart schools in the United States, had robust programs for the girls to serve the poor. I and the other RSCJ who were headmistresses believed that our students had to learn to build bridges across social classes. We also believed that the gospel teaching "Those to whom much is given, from whom much is required" (Luke 12:48), as well as the adage "Only give your best to the poor" had to be seared deeply into our students' hearts and consciences.
>
> We raised millions of dollars for financial aid and offered workshops to help faculty support diversity. But we headmistresses, then all RSCJ,

> running twenty-three Network schools across the country, often thought of ourselves as "the dinosaurs." As the Society aligned itself with the Church's "preferential option for the poor," we felt that by remaining in school administration maybe we were on the wrong side of the gospels. A watershed moment came when the RSCJ heads met with Concepción Camacho (Concha), RSCJ, our superior general. Margaret (Peggy) Brown, RSCJ, a senior head of school speaking for us all, looked intently at Concha and said, "Tell us Concha. Are our schools following the mission of the Society of the Sacred Heart? If not, we can plan ahead ...." Concha shot back: "Our schools are central to the life of the Society. Keep them strong, continue your efforts for social justice and direct service to those in need...." That meeting gave us a new life. We sharpened the Goals and Criteria and aimed at developing direct reciprocal relationships between schools and institutions supporting people in need. Vatican II opened our eyes to embrace the world. It also firmly embedded in our hearts the call of the Church to continually open the windows, to let the wind of the Holy Spirit, sometimes more like a violent storm, rush through our hearts, hallways, parishes, schools, and communities so as to bring fresh air and new hope.

This reflection through the lens of one RSCJ captures some of the tensions felt at the time. There was hope and pain, courage and fear, confusion and clarity. Catholics in parishes had the same mix of feelings, as the local churches experimented with the vernacular, with guitar Masses, with receiving communion in the hand, with lay ministers. Religious and laity alike were being called to deepen and renew their faith even as they were called to move forward. The practices that had been in place were in transition at every level, but fortunately, the Sacred Heart schools had been strengthened by the mission-focused philosophy of education expressed in the Goals and Criteria.

1. Alice McDonell,RSCJ,and Mary Fenner on “Orange Hat Patrol” in Sursum Corda during the height of the crack epidemic of the late 1980s.

2. Anne Montgomery, RSCJ, demonstrating for peace with Elmer Maas (left) and Daniel Berrigan, SJ, (right) in 1980

3. Rosemary Bearss, RSCJ, with children at the Barnyard Neighborhood Community Center in Coconut Grove, Florida, in the early 1980s.

4. The mural in Plaza Betances in the heart of the Casa del Sol neighborhood in Boston. Many RSCJ, including Carol Putnam and Muriel Heide, were deeply involved in the activities of this neighborhood. An imprint of their profession crosses can be found where they pressed them into the clay of the mural.

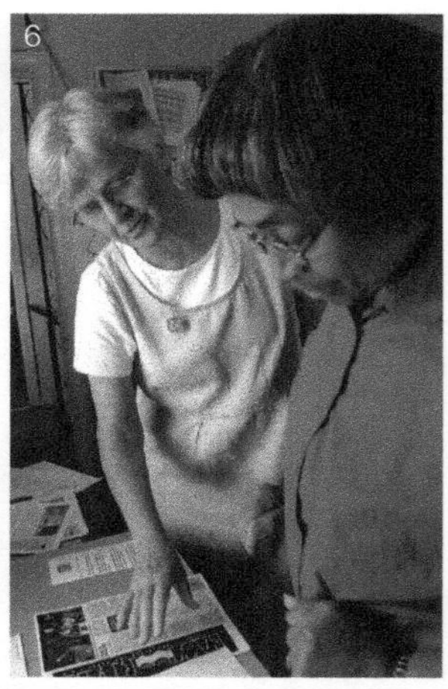

5. Annette Zipple, RSCJ, with students from the Sacred Heart Enrichment Program (SHEP) in Detroit in the 1970s.

6. Betsy Hartson, RSCJ, with volunteer Jeannette Yates at Living Wages, an educational program for adults that she co-founded with Bob Crittenden in Washington, D.C., in the late 1990s.

7. Marie McHugh, RSCJ, and Ronnie, the little brother of Irma Dillard, RSCJ, in 1968 in East Palo Alto where the RSCJ were present for many years.

8. Workshop in Preaching and Music held at Catholic Theological Union in Chicago, July 18-29, 1986.

9. Michael Madrigal, (left) administrator of St. Joseph Mission Church; Billy Meza (center) known as "Uncle Billy," a spiritual leader among the people, and Marianna Torrano, RSCJ, in late 1990s. They worked as a team to serve the spiritual needs of the people on the Soboba Indian Reservation in San Jacinto, California.

10. Helen O'Regan, RSCJ, from the US and Mary Roe, RSCJ, from the England-Wales Province participate in the celebration of the 50th anniversary of the Uganda/Kenya Province. The Province of Uganda was formed in 1962 and Kenya followed in 1973.

11. Gwen Hoeffel, RSCJ, with some children from her English class in Nagoya. The mother is Remi Yamazaki with her daughter, Seno with fan. Sister Hoeffel was in Japan from 1965 until 2014.

12. Joan Ewing, RSCJ, and Mike Hoffman, RSCJ, at the Thensted Center in Grand Coteau, Louisiana, in the 1980s

13. L to R: Ms Donna Schneider, Libby Hoye, RSCJ, Mary Gen Smyth, RSCJ, in front of Abba House of Prayer in Albany, New York.

14. At Sprout Creek Farm, students learned to live in harmony with animals and the land.

Works of Mercy

When cloister was lifted in 1964, and RSCJ were able to have more influence over the kind of work they did, a number of women chose to engage in ministries that put them in direct contact with low-income and marginalized populations. For some, like Alice McDonell, RSCJ, who had been a nurse before she entered the Society, it was a chance to return to a beloved profession that she thought she had given up when she decided to become Religious of the Sacred Heart. Others experienced a new call, inspired by urgent social needs. In preparing to respond to this call, some, like Annette Zipple, RSCJ, who worked for decades in the poorest neighborhoods of Detroit, sought professional training in social work. Often, the works they did expressed one or more of the corporal or spiritual works of mercy; that is, caring for the bodily and spiritual needs of others.

One of the Society's earliest ventures into direct service with poor persons began immediately after Special Chapter 1967, which called on RSCJ to follow founder Madeleine Sophie Barat's wish that the sisters give attention to the poor. Claire Krim, RSCJ, rented a storefront in Harlem where she established the Fifth Avenue Community Center, a crisis center for the people of the neighborhood, especially youth. At the time, she was head of Duchesne Residence School on New York City's Upper East Side, a two-year program for young women, and she saw the center as a place where these relatively affluent students could provide social services. Sister Krim died shortly after beginning the Fifth Avenue center. Agnes Donovan, RSCJ, replaced her and several RSCJ from the Convent of the Sacred Heart on 91st Street helped out. As the activities of the center multiplied, it became clear that a fulltime director was needed, and after some years, Leontine O'Gorman, RSCJ, was named to this post by the New York provincial team.

Sister O'Gorman introduced educational programs that prepared gifted elementary school children of Harlem for good high schools, provided employment opportunities for inner city youth, and offered addiction treatment for prisoners to enable them to avoid repetition of criminal behavior on release. The Jobs Education Development Initiative (JEDI), a summer program, provided work experience and coaching for youngsters with few opportunities. Sister O'Gorman was talented in raising money to sustain these endeavors and in getting citizens of New York to staff the projects and serve as trustees,

Different Living Arrangements

Some of these pioneers lived and worked with lay colleagues rather than in RSCJ residences. Sister O'Gorman sometimes lived with the people she served in the crumbling tenements near the Fifth Avenue Community Center. Others, like Carol Bialock, RSCJ, decided to live with radical Christian communities like the Catholic Worker, which provided a bed and a meal to anyone in need. Still others were part of a small RSCJ community in a poor neighborhood where they found ministries nearby. For instance, in 1974, several RSCJ created the 49th Street Community in the Hell's Kitchen neighborhood of New York City, where Chris Webber, RSCJ, worked with runaway youth at Covenant House and Joan Kirby, RSCJ, advocated for affordable housing with Housing Conservation Coordinators. A few years later, two RSCJ, Rosa Orjuela, and Bienvenida Velez, founded a small community in LaBelle, Florida, where they were soon joined by Sisters Mercedes Posada and Madeleine Desloge. All of these RSCJ originally worked at Our Lady Queen of Heaven Parish, as did Muriel Cameron, RSCJ, when she served in LaBelle several years later. Others, like Marie-Louise Wolfington, RSCJ, who lived there in the 1990s, found work with local non-profits like Habitat for Humanity.

Many RSCJ who felt this call to serve the poor did volunteer work with established agencies or parishes. For example, Louise Lundergan worked with St. Vincent de Paul Society in San Francisco, counseling people dealing with substance abuse. Rosemary Statt in San Jose, California; Betsy Hartson in Washington, D.C.; and Bonnie Kearney in Chicago, staffed homeless shelters run by Catholic Charities. Margaret Phelan in San Francisco and Los Angeles provided services to newly arrived immigrants, and Julie Yachtis and Mary Brady served as social workers for various agencies in Washington, D.C., and upstate New York.

Three RSCJ, Flavia Augustine, Margaret Burke and Nancy Kane, continued to work in formal education while working with the Benedictine sisters at the Howard Area Community Center in Rogers Park, Chicago, to provide help with job placement, GED classes and counseling. Virginia McMonagle, RSCJ, divided her time in her later years between her work at the University of San Diego and volunteering at *Nos Petits Frères et Soeurs*, an orphanage in Haiti.

Prison Ministries

Although each of the RSCJ mentioned above was breaking new ground, the ministries of those who worked in prisons were often the most challenging. People generally could easily accept the idea of women religious wanting to provide food, shelter, health care or education to those most in need; it was harder for some to imagine their former teachers and school administrators interacting with people convicted of crimes.

The number of RSCJ who worked with individuals affected by the criminal justice system is greater than one might think. It includes Lorette (Retsy) Piper who worked at Martin House in Trenton, New Jersey; Patricia Barrett, who worked with the St. Louis County juvenile court in Missouri; Margaret Burke, who assisted at the federal women's prison in Dwight, Illinois; and Margaret (Margie) Conroy, who worked with prisoners in Uganda. Others were Barbara Cooper in Somerset County, New Jersey; Ann Conroy, who tutored women in a maximum security prison in Bedford, New York; Joan Gannon, who visited prisoners and helped found Newport Citizens Concerned about Corrections as part of her ministry at St. Barnabas Parish in Portsmouth, Rhode Island; Rosemary Dowd, who worked with prisoners in Illinois and Louisiana; and Clare Pratt who volunteered as a liturgist at Regina Coeli prison when she was in Rome.

Two of the women mentioned above expressed in writing what their motivation was for doing this work and how they reconciled it with the educational mission of the Society. Their stories are told in greater detail below.

Patricia Barrett, RSCJ

In the 1960s and 1970s, there was a growing sense that many who were convicted of crimes and incarcerated were also victims of social injustices related to poverty, skin color, or inability to pay for bail or legal representation. Sister Barrett, who was working at Maryville College in St. Louis in the 1950s, teaching the papal social encyclicals, was one of the first to respond to this social concern. In 1984 she wrote:

> I did not come out of any theology in my poverty ministry, but was motivated and guided in my teaching and actions by the developing social doctrines of the Church from Leo XIII to Paul VI .... With Maryville's move [from the City of St. Louis] to St. Louis County, and the heightened civil rights activity of the late 1950s and '60s, I began to move into practical projects that were expanded with the easing of cloister.... In the mid- 1960s, Maryville's political science department initiated a citizenship training seminar for the residents of a notoriously bad housing project called Pruitt-Igoe. Most of the residents were Black, and many were eager to take advantage of opportunities that came their way. CITAS (Citizenship Training Seminar) was sponsored by the public housing authority, welfare, the North Side Team Ministry and Father John Shocklee of Saint Bridget's Catholic Church in the inner city. Participants ... met twice a week at night in the Crunden Public Library. The curriculum consisted in a comprehensive survey of the essentials of American government .... A surprising number of CITAS graduates became leaders in the Black community during the 1960s and 1970s.[74]

Sister Barrett worked for HDC (Human Development Corporation) in St. Louis, which sent her to the city jail. There, along with Maryville students whom she encouraged to volunteer, she taught math, English, and reading to female prisoners. She developed some lasting friendships with the women. She also belonged to a creative group at the state penitentiary for men in Jefferson City, Missouri, called Lifers Incorporated. Then, in the 1970s, Maryville introduced a criminal justice program which enabled law enforcement personnel to earn a bachelor's degree with criminal justice as a major. Sister Barrett taught many of these classes off campus at local police stations and other public venues.

Rosemary Dowd, RSCJ

Sister Dowd began her prison ministry as a volunteer for the county jail in Waukegan, Illinois, when she was working at Woodlands Academy in Lake Forest in the early 1960s. Of this experience, she wrote:

> One evening, Holy Thursday, I returned home from my two hours in the jail visiting room and went to sign our *prie dieu* list for adoration. The heading was: 'Can't you spend one hour with Me?' I knew absolutely I had just spent two hours with the Lord in that jail. From that moment more than forty-three years ago, my desire for this ministry has only intensified, and my gratitude to God and the Society for allowing me to pursue the 'second vocation' is boundless.[75]

She went on to minister full time with incarcerated men and women in New Orleans as a deputy sheriff and chaplain in Orleans Parish, and in Chicago as a social worker and chaplain at the Cook County Jail. She would meet and pray with them, find out what they needed, contact family members, bring them books and magazines. She listened to them without judgment. She shared her experiences with her community, with students at Sacred Heart schools, with alumnae who often wondered at how their former dean of students had turned to this ministry. Even when her eyesight was failing, she found ways to get to the jail, to be with people she counted among her friends.

In her early years in prison ministry, Sister Dowd used to wonder how that work fit with her vow of education. However, she gradually came to understand that as a prison chaplain her job was to "draw out" (*educere* in Latin) the goodness that is within each person, no matter what he or she may have done. "I think that if a person who did not know before of the transformative power of God's love learns that lesson in jail, it will have been worth his incarceration. Of course, I would definitely prefer that they learn it elsewhere!"

Corporate Ministries

One of the concerns raised by some when RSCJ left the schools to work with poor and marginalized populations was that the congregation would lose its visibility. The fact that RSCJ were no longer in habit and needed to find paying jobs meant that they did, literally, blend in with the general population. However, when a group of RSCJ joined together to support a ministry to some marginalized or underserved group, their efforts were often more visible. Rosemary (Wickie) Sheehan, RSCJ, and many others provided after school and other educational programs for low-income children at the Carver Center in Portchester, New York. Two RSCJ, Sarah (Sally) Brennan and Nancy Finn, together with Sheridan Road teachers and alumnae/i, worked to provide shelter for homeless women at Casa Esperanza in Chicago. Helen Carroll, Mary McGann, Irma Dillard, and Gertrude (Trudy) Patch, all RSCJ, served in a variety of ways at Our Lady of Lourdes Parish at Hunters Point in San Francisco. Sister McGann continued with the community for fourteen years, and in the process published a book on the gospel music tradition of the parish.[76]

One well-known corporate ministry was the Thensted Center in Grand Coteau, Louisiana. Named for Cornelius J. Thensted, SJ, the Thensted Center was founded in 1974 by Margaret (Mike) Hoffman, RSCJ. As a registered nurse, Sister Hoffman could clearly see the many needs of the largely African American community in the small, rural town of Grand Coteau. She spent many months on her motorbike visiting the families and isolated elderly residents, talking with them about their lives and getting their ideas about what would be helpful. Eventually, with a staff of two laywomen from the community and a host of volunteers, the center began to offer recreational and educational programs for young people, a thrift store, a food bank, a money-management program, and meeting spaces for local groups like Al-Anon and the Boy Scouts. During the summer, a large above-ground swimming pool provided welcome relief from the southern heat for all the local children and volunteers from Sacred Heart schools, who showed up each year to help with the summer enrichment programs. Over the years, many RSCJ came and spent time working and volunteering at the Thensted Center, most notably Betty Renard, RSCJ, who, after Sister Hoffman, and in partnership with a dedicated staff, was the RSCJ most deeply committed to the thriving of this ministry. The presence of the Academy of the Sacred Heart just down the road allowed for a mutually beneficial partnership on many levels.[77]

Recognized as a place for unconditional welcome and life-giving support, Thensted Center was named the 2012 Agency of the Year by United Way of St. Landry-Evangeline, and in 2022, KM Strategies Group (KMSG), a social impact advisory firm based in Washington, D.C., announced it was awarding the Thensted Center its $45,000 social impact award.

Another high-profile corporate ministry that began attracting RSCJ in the mid-1980s was the Little Sisters of the Assumption Family Health Center in

East Harlem, New York. By the time Judy Garson, RSCJ, became director of the center in 1984, it was a thriving agency providing health care, education, emergency food and clothing to over 1,700 families living in and around Spanish Harlem. Religious women from five different congregations collaborated with laymen and laywomen to staff the center with funding from foundations and wealthy benefactors.

Over the course of the twenty-three years that Sister Garson served as director of the health center, more than a dozen members of the Society of the Sacred Heart worked there. Some RSCJ, like Eve Kavanagh, Betty Renard, Helen O'Regan, Stephany Veluz and Nancy Murphy served on the nursing staff. Others, like Judy Cagney and Marie (Maisie) Lufkin, used their professional expertise in finance or education.

Sister Garson knew little about serving the poor when she was invited by the provincial of the Little Sisters to become the director, but, as she explained in an interview with *Heart* magazine in 2007,[78] she had visited the Society's provinces worldwide as part of her service on the General Council of the Society of the Sacred Heart in Rome, and had seen firsthand the often oppressive effects of U.S. policy. She came home determined to serve disadvantaged people. "I learned that there is a way of being a health care worker, a social worker, a teacher, that is both educational and empowering," she said.

Concluding Thoughts

This chapter has revisited some of the ministries of RSCJ who stood out for their direct service to poor and marginalized people during the years after Vatican II.

Sometimes these women began their work of direct service with a clear vision drawn from social analysis and were simultaneously engaged in service and advocacy. For instance, Sister Piper, who worked at Martin House, was also a member of groups like Pax Christi and the Coalition for Nuclear Disarmament.

Some of the sisters who started out simply doing direct service with poor people eventually began to ask structural questions that led them to further educate themselves and incorporate a deeper theological and political dimension to their work. For example, Sister Hoffman, after years of working with the poor as a nurse, went back to earn a master's degree from the School of Applied Theology in Berkeley, California, with an emphasis on ministry to those who are poor. Many others who might logically be included in greater depth in this chapter are only briefly mentioned.

There were many other RSCJ who found great satisfaction and meaning in living out the gospel imperatives to visit the sick, feed the hungry and clothe the naked, which they did with great courage and dedication in poor neighborhoods across this country: Juana Resto in the South End of Boston; Helen Costello in

Atherton, California; Ana Ospina at Sacred Heart Parish in New York City, and Ana Soto in Miami.

In each case, and in so many others throughout this book, we see women who either moved from the social justice teachings of the Church to practical application or, conversely, moved from understanding themselves to be the hands and feet of Christ in service to the poor to realizing that raising their voices in political advocacy for those among whom they lived and worked was also a way to serve. We see RSCJ using their education and their compassionate hearts to bring a measure of justice to those on the margins, always with the educator's desire to lead the individual to discover his or her own dignity as a child of God.

Community Organizing

Introduction

Two powerful forces combined in the 1960s to draw many women religious in the United States into poor neighborhoods. In January 1964, United States President Lyndon Johnson, responding to a national poverty rate around 19 percent, announced his "War on Poverty." A year later, the Second Vatican Council in *Gaudium et Spes* called on Catholics to address the "hopes, the grief and anguish of the people of our time, especially those who are poor or afflicted."[79]

Members of the Society of the Sacred Heart in the United States, young and old, from every geographic region and socio-economic background, shared a sense that they were being called to respond to these signs of the times. While some continued to live in their large convent communities, a few set out to live in low-income neighborhoods as they turned from teaching in classrooms to work in parishes, agencies, or schools that served the poor.

Between 1967 and 1979, across the five provinces in the United States, at least eight such small-group communities formed. These were Sursum Corda in Washington, D.C.; Casa del Sol in the South End of Boston; Naranja/Indiantown/Labelle in Florida; Saint Rita's Parish in Detroit; Saint Francis of Assisi Parish in East Palo Alto, California; the Green Street Projects in Albany, New York; 118th Street in East Harlem, New York City; and the 49th Street and 51st Street Communities in Hell's Kitchen, New York City. This chapter will consider in depth three of these communities: Sursum Corda, Casa del Sol, and East Palo Alto, offering evidence for why the RSCJ left their former ministries, how they dealt with the challenges they faced, and whether their efforts made a difference. The stories will focus on events between 1968 and 1978, when these communities were just getting started, although in later years several other RSCJ engaged in formal community organizing, including Marina Hernandez, who worked in San Diego, and Mary Bernstein, who worked in Chicago.

Motivation and Challenges

Clearly, the documents coming out of Vatican II had a profound effect on all vowed religious who were reading them, as did the document *Justice in the World* issued by the World Synod of Catholic Bishops in 1971.[80] Many members of the Society were also acquainted with the writings of Brazilian educator Paulo Freire (*Pedagogy of the Oppressed*, 1970) and Peruvian Dominican Gustavo Gutiérrez (*A Theology of Liberation*, 1971), as well as with examples of individuals like Dorothy Day, founder of the Catholic Worker movement in 1933. Some had marched from Selma to Montgomery, Alabama, with civil rights leader Dr. Martin Luther King, Jr., in 1965, and others had joined in the anti-Vietnam War movement in the late 1960s and early 1970s. Social change was in the air, and many RSCJ were deeply hopeful that a more just social order was possible.

Some young RSCJ who went to Rome to make their final vows in 1969 under Hélène Dessain, RSCJ, found it hard to manage their frustration with the slow pace of change. As Rosa Carbonell, RSCJ, writes in her life of María Josefa Bultó, "There were probanists who did not accept some of the orientations of the probation mistress, thinking them obsolete."[81]

But it was not only the young who were impatient for radical change. Perhaps one of the most moving accounts of this longing for social change in an older RSCJ is found is a 1967 letter from Faine McMullen, RSCJ, to Betty Sweeney, RSCJ, provincial of the Washington Province, asking for permission to live outside of community. Sister McMullen, who was 54 years old at the time, wrote:

> My way is this—and as I expound it, I beg you to give it your most understanding consideration, for this is not caprice—I am deadly in earnest. I ask you for permission to exclaustrate for two years, [82] starting on or about July 30, 1967, for the purpose of devoting all my time and energy and personal presence and witness in a situation which will identify me directly and absolutely with the poor. I would live with the poor as a poor person in Boston's South End and/or Roxbury and support myself by work that would be a direct application of political science to life. My intention is to seek an understanding of the problems … race and poverty particularly. By living where the problem is and by working through the Commonwealth [of Massachusetts] or a public agency dealing with the problems, I would achieve an understanding of the problems and of what can be done about them in a way that thirteen years in our classrooms have failed to produce. At the end of two years, I hope to offer the Society my understanding of the politics of poverty gained experientially from the inside out.

Carol Putnam, RSCJ, one of the founders of Casa del Sol, echoed Sister McMullen's intuition that living directly with the poor was the only way to truly understand how to help without inadvertently imposing solutions. In an interview in 1970, Sister Putnam was asked what Casa del Sol was trying to accomplish. The interviewer noted that her response reflected the mission of one of Casa del Sol's funding sources, the newly formed Catholic Campaign for Human Development. Its motto was "helping the poor help themselves." A grant of $7,000 from the Catholic Campaign, plus a $3,000 gift from the Society, enabled the sisters to carry out a pilot project. "Our first goal is respect for the people," Sister Putnam said. "'We don't want to talk about the lives of the people on the street as though we are trying to do something for them. We are living here, and what we do we will do as members of the community."

While a longing for social justice was a common denominator in all these early communities in poor neighborhoods, there was also a shared feeling of intense joy in the work and a deeply felt affection for the people among whom the RSCJ lived. In a letter written at the time of her Golden Jubilee, marking fifty years since her final vows, Sister Margaret Reilly described her life in East Palo Alto in 1970:

> The people at once opened to us their hearts and their homes. We were showered with gifts of eggs, fruit and vegetables from their gardens. They stopped us in the streets to say "Thank you for coming to live with us." We are deeply attached to our little mission and very happy in our work. My religious life has always known a deep contentment, but never before so great as this.

Of the three neighborhoods explored in this chapter, two were predominantly Black, and the other was largely Latinx and Spanish-speaking. While many of the sisters brought useful skills with them such as nursing, law, or teaching, most of them were white and came from upper-middle-class families. They sometimes lacked the "street sense" necessary to navigate low-income neighborhoods. They wanted to develop the capacity and strengths of the people they lived among, but it was sometimes hard for them not to automatically take the lead. They also found themselves having to cook and organize their prayer lives without the support of a large institution. Their stories reveal determination and resilience in the face of challenge.

Sursum Corda Village

In the early 1960s, urban renewal projects brought drastic change to inner city neighborhoods across the United States. In Washington, D.C., one of the neighborhoods slated for extensive demolition included an area surrounding Gonzaga College High School on North Capitol Street. The Jesuits, wanting to engage the low-income residents in the neighborhood in the rehabilitation planning, worked with them in responding to an invitation from the city to sponsor, design, and construct new affordable housing in the area. Eugene Stewart, a successful lawyer and a Georgetown alumnus, formed the non-profit Sursum Corda, Inc. Its board of directors included two other Georgetown alumni, Richard McCooey and Frank McManus, as well as neighborhood residents, Jesuits, Sisters of Notre Dame de Namur, and others with relevant expertise. The Latin words *sursum corda* mean "lift up your hearts," and those working on the project hoped it would become a model mixed-income neighborhood.

Father Horace McKenna, SJ, an older Jesuit who was much loved by the low-income residents of the neighborhood, also happened to be the cousin of an RSCJ, Kate McDonnell. He invited her to consider moving, along with other RSCJ, into one of Sursum Corda's new six-bedroom units. In the fall of 1969,

Sister McDonnell, who had been teaching at the college level but had a deep interest in housing issues, and Alice McDonell, who had been a public health nurse, were among the first RSCJ to move into 1124 McKenna Walk. They were soon joined by four other RSCJ, Fredericka Cartwright and Juliet Cozzi, who created programs for the children, and Elizabeth Antisdale, then in her 80s, who volunteered in the community library. In 1971, Gertrude Cosenke, RSCJ joined the group and spent four years reaching out to adults in the neighborhood, getting to know their needs and their hopes.

The composition of the community changed frequently during the first four years. Sisters Cartwright and Cozzi both left the Society. Sister Antisdale retired. But others were eager to take their places. Grace Butler, RSCJ, came in 1972 and worked in the urban schools of the Archdiocese of Washington. In 1974, Diane Roche, then an RSCJ candidate, took over the work with the children and adults, and Sister McMullen, having earned a law degree, arrived and accepted a position with Neighborhood Legal Services, providing legal help to people who would not otherwise be able to afford it. That same year, Sister McDonnell received a grant from the Department of Housing and Urban Development (HUD) to start up a non-profit corporation, Housing Counselling Services, Inc., to help low-income people hold on to their homes.

Because Sursum Corda was within walking distance of the United States Capitol, political engagement seemed a natural fit for RSCJ feeling a call to work for systemic change. In response to this call, Mary O'Callaghan, RSCJ, joined the community and began lobbying for various justice issues on Capitol Hill.

From 1974 until 1980, the community remained basically stable, with additional RSCJ volunteering to work at the development during summers.[83] The religious were united in their efforts to live in solidarity with their neighbors, reflecting their shared understanding that this was the best way for them to live out the Society's charism to discover and reveal the heart of Christ in the heart of the world. Since they were also committed to working for systemic change, they collaborated with groups like Network Lobby for Catholic Social Justice, the Center of Concern, and the Community for Creative Non-violence.

Unfortunately, within the first few years, the dream of Sursum Corda as a poor people's paradise evaporated. The rents had been deliberately set low in an effort to make the housing affordable, but rising utility costs and unforeseen maintenance problems led to increasing debt. The management company was not used to overseeing low-income properties and did not carefully screen new tenants. As social problems escalated, middle-income families moved out and Sursum Corda began to be seen as a troubled property. The beautiful landscaped courtyards, effectively hidden from the police who patrolled the main streets in cars, devolved into dangerous drug markets at night. Bullet holes appeared in a door of the car belonging to the sisters and even pierced the plexiglass kitchen window.

This roller coaster ride of raised expectations and dashed hopes continued throughout the entire forty years of Sursum Corda's existence. Each time a new law or a new drug threatened to destroy the community, the tenants would respond with creativity and determination. The residents of Sursum Corda had been organized and involved even before all the units were occupied. They served on the committee that designed the units, and they hoped that one day they could own their houses.

Several strong leaders emerged among community residents, including Mary Judd, the mother of a large, stable family; Alverta Munlyn, a community organizer from the Center City Community Corporation; and Robert Wood, who worked at the Government Printing Office. Sister Roche partnered with these leaders to develop after-school programs, publish a newsletter, and improve management of the property. Together they negotiated with HUD to avoid foreclosure, and they banded together with other tenant groups to learn community organizing tactics that could help them in working with government officials and attracting social services to the neighborhood. [84] During the worst of the crack epidemic, Sister McDonell, who was then in her eighties, regularly patrolled the streets with other senior citizens wearing an orange hat and carrying a walkie-talkie. Eventually, the tenants attracted support from the Ford Foundation, the Campaign for Human Development, and HUD. A flexible subsidy loan from HUD enabled converting the property from rental to co-op in 1992, in the process giving the residents a modest realization of their dream of home ownership.

Casa del Sol

Casa del Sol was the name given to a vibrant and creative community of RSCJ and lay people in the South End of Boston during the 1960s and 70s. The RSCJ most directly responsible for the formation of Casa del Sol was Sister Putnam, who left a detailed account of the early days of this initiative, from which the following narrative is taken.

In the late 1960s, Boston's Hispanic community began to increase rapidly. A few organizations responded to the basic needs of this largely Puerto Rican and poverty-stricken population. However, visits to any of the Hispanic neighborhoods revealed many homebound women whose lives were restricted to preparing meals, listening to Spanish programs on the radio, and gazing out the windows of rat-infested tenements.

In response to the needs of these women, Susan Halligan, RSCJ, and Sister Putnam decided to establish a service program for residents in Boston's South End. They began their search for housing, funding, and collaborators in January of 1971. They visited Father Ernesto Serino at the Cardinal Cushing Center for the Spanish Speaking and received warm encouragement. They asked advice of

Israel Feliciano and Philip Bradley of the Emergency Tenants' Council, and after much searching, they found a suitable old four-story building at 10 Pembroke Street.

Prospective collaborators appeared too. Patricia O'Reilly, a Newton College alumna, spoke Spanish and had worked in the earthquake area in Peru; Patricia Blanchette and Jane Dubois had been Church Extension Volunteers in New Mexico; Mary Ann Sabetti and Fraeleen Curtis were eager to serve. The group was augmented by Nancy Looker, then a novice in the Society. This group met together ahead of time to discuss goals and a basic philosophy. The philosophy and strategy were simple: share the life and vicissitudes of the people and listen to their expression of their needs. Goals included setting up a program for women as both an outgrowth of their own expression of need and a mutual collaboration.

The initial phase of the program began on August 22, 1971, when four of the group moved into the house at 10 Pembroke Street. By September 9, all eight members were present and able to experience the life of the block where almost 500 Puerto Ricans lived and where there was a high rate of broken homes, unemployment, drugs, gambling, thefts, and fires. It was a block judged by the police to be one of the worst in the city.

The top floors and basement of the house had not been used for a number of years, so much cleaning and renovating needed to be done. Everyone pitched in, often working late into the night. Since there were no curtains, neighbors saw what was going on and soon came with offers of help. Men gave whole days to painting while women scrubbed and washed as if the house belonged to them too. Not only did the house become habitable; it developed a personality, and it needed a name. After fielding a number of suggestions, the group came up with a name that seemed to embody the spirit of the place: Casa del Sol: House of the Sun.

Development of the program was slowed by insufficient funds to provide anyone with a full-time salary. But this proved to be an asset. All the RSCJ secured low-paying teaching jobs in bilingual and high school equivalency programs and in a nearby parochial school. Their regular coming and going from these jobs in the community allowed them to become part of the scene.

The first activity was one that had not been planned for: development of a food cooperative to offset the high prices and poor quality of food in the local supermarkets. Through the United South End Food Cooperative, people were able to purchase fruits and vegetables, eggs, meat, cheese, and bread of very good quality at an almost 50 percent cost reduction.

During October and November, besides doing regular tasks and working at the co-op, members of Casa del Sol responded to frequent requests to take mothers and children to the clinic and to act as interpreters at the welfare office and the Boston Housing Authority. They accompanied tenants to visits to their landlords to protest when there was no heat. On one occasion, they donated blood for a young man who had been badly injured in an auto accident. Little by little, these informal contacts and human responses led to mutual trust and acceptance.

The first informal invitation to the house to neighborhood residents was for an evening conference on lead poisoning held at Casa del Sol on December 6, 1971. Staff members of Boston Children's Hospital and the local clinic explained in Spanish the symptoms and dangers of lead poisoning. Although it was dark, rainy and cold, there was an excellent turnout of parents and children. All agreed that, while medical groups can help people to discover the effects of lead poisoning, it is the housing authority that can get at the cause by testing the paint in the old houses of the South End and preventing the harm at its source.

The women were enthusiastic about attending classes in languages (Spanish and English), budgeting, and homemaking. With an average educational level of fifth grade, they were alert and eager to learn. The classes began in January with a group of about eight mothers. January also saw the transfer of a cooking class from a location that had only one hot plate to the large bright kitchen of Casa del Sol. A group of ten Puerto Rican women were taught by other neighborhood residents to use government surplus foods.

Plans were made for the following year. The Massachusetts Department of Education provided $2,000 through its Division of Occupational Education. The local Campaign for Human Development gave $4,800 for a teaching assistant, and the Raskob Foundation gave $7,000 to provide day care services for the students' children. Thus, the program was able to initiate a clerical and bookkeeping component and continue English and high school equivalency classes in Spanish. New residents came to the Casa del Sol household: a young man with experience in Latin America and two RSCJ, Thaïs Ascanio and Lisa Fitzgerald.

In 1973, the school became incorporated as the Casa del Sol Educational Program, Inc., a private nonprofit educational institution. The budget for the second year of business training was $54,000. Mark Delamano and Muriel Heide, RSCJ, joined the staff, and the program took firmer shape.

From the outset, the Society of the Sacred Heart took a strong and supportive interest in the development of Casa del Sol. Two successive loans of $10,000 and $15,000 helped to carry the project through times of financial stress. An exchange of services project linked students at Newton Country Day School of the Sacred Heart with elderly residents of the South End who needed help with activities such as shopping or bathing, or wanted someone to read to them, or just visit. In return these older people shared their memories of the past, which proved to be an enriching experience for the young people. This service to the elderly was continued in later years by Sister Heide in conjunction with campus ministry programs at Boston College.

A 1982 article in the *RSCJ Newsletter* celebrating the tenth anniversary of Casa del Sol states:

> Since 1971, Casa del Sol has been growing steadily. The yearly budget has grown from $54,000 in the 1973-1974 fiscal year to over $350,000 in 1980. In the past five years, Casa del Sol has served over 3000 students in the areas of literacy training, basic education, training for entry-level business careers, college preparation (including the opportunity to earn up to thirty hours of college credit), and employment assistance services. In addition, Casa del Sol offers classes in multicultural arts and cultural enrichment programs for the community at large and for students in three of Boston's public schools.

Real estate records show that the house at 10 Pembroke Street was bought by the City of Boston and torn down as part of their redevelopment plan. In 1975, two new communities of RSCJ opened in the South End. One opened at 20 Paseo Aguadilla in the newly built Villa Victoria neighborhood, and the other was at 437 Shawmut Avenue. In addition to the RSCJ mentioned previously, those involved included Clare Pratt, Maggie Kilduff, Eve Kavanagh, Jean Bartunek, Connie Cummiskey, Grail McMullen, Mercedes Posada, Juana Resto, and Carlota Duarte.

East Palo Alto, California

The following story of the RSCJ community in East Palo Alto is taken from a narrative written by Irma Dillard, RSCJ, in response to requests for material for this book. Sister Dillard actually found her vocation through her interactions with the RSCJ who were part of this community.

In 1960, East Palo Alto was a small, predominantly Black community surrounded by richer, mostly white San Francisco and San Jose suburbs. East Palo Alto remained an unincorporated area governed by San Mateo County. Its workforce found employment outside the area, and residents had a limited voice in policies that affected them. The widening of Highway 101 in the 1950s, for example, eliminated forty-five of the community's leading businesses. Menlo Park and Palo Alto annexed 25 percent of the community in the 1960s, depriving it of both population and property tax revenue. Residents were also heavily taxed for county services, such as sanitation, water, and recreation.

To counter this second-class status, the people of East Palo Alto attempted to incorporate five times between 1931 and 1981. In the 1968 attempt, some local Black leaders even tried to rename the city Nairobi, after Kenya's capital city! They were finally successful at incorporating in 1983. Yet, despite that success, East Palo Alto suffered continued population loss. The area had become the largest African American community on the peninsula, but increasing white flight, and flight of members of the Black middle class, led to a growing crime rate spurred on by drug sales and use.

By the late 1960s, East Palo Alto was in turmoil and trying to find its identity apart from Menlo Park. African Americans were deep into the Black movement and making it known that they were black and proud. Around that time, the Precious Blood Fathers moved their provincial house to Saint Francis of Assisi parish, and the Holy Family Sisters were planning to leave. The priests began talking to Beth Nothomb, RSCJ, then provincial of the Society's California Province.

Marie McHugh, RSCJ, held a series of meetings with the Precious Blood priests and the parishioners of St. Francis of Assisi. She wanted to hear from the people, to learn what they wanted and needed. It became clear that education, religious education for young people (CCD), early childhood education, home visits and adult bible study were top priorities. The RSCJ worked closely with Fathers Richard Griever, provincial, and Anthony Gamble, pastor; and two seminarians, Bill Finn and Chris Sandholdt, to design programs for the parish. At this time, the predominately African American parish had a growing population of Hispanics, the majority of whom came from Mexico— "Chicanos" in California. The parish also included a few Italian families and older Irish widows who remained after the white flight of the early 1960s, as well as a few Japanese families. There was a clear message: East Palo Alto was being ignored, and there was a great need for education, resources, and spiritual boosting.

Sister McHugh went to visit and speak with the other RSCJ in the United States who had chosen to live and work directly with the economically poor, with a goal of gaining a deeper understanding of their situations. In 1969 Sister McHugh and two other RSCJ, Sistina Pietrobono and Margaret Reilly, moved into what came to be known as "the little green house," a newly renovated green two-story house that had been given to the parish by the Kavanaugh family. In 1970, Linda Hayward, RSCJ, joined the community, followed by Juanita (Jenny) Hills, RSCJ, who came to provide more assistance to the Spanish-speaking parishioners.

In 1970, Sister Reilly decided to celebrate her Golden Jubilee at the parish, and many parishioners attended. Sister Reilly had asked her sisters to come in habit, and although most had stopped wearing the habit, they all accommodated her request. It was quite a sight, and a real witness to religious life.

Early education was vitally important to the African American and Mexican American families, and RSCJ played supportive roles. Sisters McHugh and Hayward began training and study in the Maria Montessori method at the University of Notre Dame in Belmont, California.[85] They began working in the Creative Montessori Learning Center on the church property in their second year. Antonia Ramos, RSCJ, joined the community in 1974 to work in an afternoon Montessori Program, and Pamela Yell, RSCJ, came from Nova Scotia to teach CCD and work with the parents. There were many other RSCJ who came during the summer months, including Theresa Teshima, Barbara Dawson, and Lucille Kramer.

In 1976, Sister McHugh left East Palo Alto to join her blood sister, Sister Helen McHugh, in teaching at the University of the Sacred Heart in Tokyo. Sister Ramos went to teach in her home country of Puerto Rico. Sisters Hayward and Pietrobono continued for another year, until 1977, when Sister Pietrobono joined the community at Oakwood, and Sister Hayward accepted a position with the Dominican Sisters at Santa Sabina Retreat Center in San Rafael. The Precious Blood seminarians moved into the little green house and continued the work until the Precious Blood Fathers pulled out of the parish a few years later. Saint Francis of Assisi became an archdiocesan parish again, and the little green house became home to a law office that provided legal assistance to the people of the area.

In 1988, Saint Francis of Assisi Parish again welcomed an RSCJ, Carmen Parrilla, who, following a training program in Marriage Encounter, came to work with couples to strengthen their marriages. She also worked with youth and visited sick people and prisoners in both East Palo Alto and Redwood City.

The Effects and the Promise

Certainly, the presence of RSCJ communities in these seven low-income neighborhoods brought some concrete benefits to the people among whom they lived. The RSCJ provided year-round programs for adults and children: tutoring, religious education, summer day camp, an afternoon Montessori program, Catholic Youth Organization activities for teenagers, Rite of Christian Initiation for Adults, Bible study, English as a second language, and a women's jail ministry. The sisters became vital to the life of the parish. They had an open-door policy and many of the groups preferred meeting in the little green house rather than in the parish hall. Prayers groups emerged and they built relationships quickly. People felt at home.

However, programs alone do not tell the whole story. More important even than programs were the tools the RSCJ offered to parishioners that they could use to advocate for themselves and build on their own gifts. The sisters also lifted people up. For the first time, the people of Saint Francis felt they mattered, that they had a voice. The RSCJ also gave the people a thirst for education. Many youth in the neighborhood were first generation Californians who would not have graduated from junior or senior high school if not for the RSCJ.

The sisters provided spiritual guidance as well. The majority of the African American families of Saint Francis came from Louisiana during the great migration in the 1940s. They brought their faith, their Catholic religion, and a deep thirst for Scripture. They had left their homes during the Jim Crow era and endured many challenges in their quest for a better life and jobs, and by faith and perseverance made a new home in East Palo Alto. The RSCJ took the time to listen and, perhaps most important, to understand the people and to get to know their culture.

The sisters ate soul food for the first time: greens and cornbread, fried chicken, ham hocks and beans and rice. They experienced Mardi Gras and Zydeco East Palo Alto style. They tasted real Mexican food and joined in the celebration for Our Lady of Guadalupe. Family was number one to the parishioners, and the sisters joined with open hearts.

The RSCJ also benefited from this intimate connection with their neighbors. While they may have arrived as well-intentioned but naïve outsiders, those who stayed the course were deeply changed. The suffering they witnessed and experienced was a powerful motivation for deep reflection. They learned to think about the local and global systems that contribute to the degradation of human beings.

Many of those who lived in these seven communities went on to found other communities that reflected the lessons they had learned. Sister Putnam left the South End of Boston to found Hope Rural School in Indiantown, Florida, and the Mecca community in California. Sister Roche built on her Sursum Corda experience to create a similar community in St. Louis. Sisters Bienvenida Velez and Rosa Orjuela brought their experience from Naranja to their work in Indiantown and then to the community in LaBelle.

Other RSCJ who worked in similar projects were motivated by what they had seen and experienced to respond by directly challenging the oppressive systems that caused such suffering. For example, Anne Montgomery, RSCJ, after time at the Green Street Community in Albany, devoted years to actions of civil disobedience in order to call attention to the dangers to the human community and the gross waste of taxpayer dollars posed by building nuclear weapons and waging war. Rose Marie Quilter, RSCJ, went on to use the experience she gained from living in Saint Rita's Parish in Detroit to join with ARISE in Alamo, Texas, a non-profit organization that fosters the empowerment of immigrant women. Oonah Ryan, RSCJ, founded Neighborhood Artisans in Detroit, a small nonprofit business that employed low-income residents and taught them skills like silk screening and graphic design.

Clearly, these early inner-city communities of RSCJ had a powerful influence on the United States Province as well. In 1992, its planning document *An Act of Hope*[86] declared:

> We choose as province to orient our life and apostolic service toward: Joining the struggle of the poor for the resources and conditions essential for human well-being, recognizing that education is central to the effort and to our vocation; Working against racism, sexism, and violence of every kind, recognizing in these forces a call to become, in truth, women who build communion.

The document goes on to state: "Choosing to join the struggle of the poor means gradually coming to act 'from within and with' rather than 'from without and for.' In addition, ... we need to "Make it our ordinary pattern, over time, to live in poor/working class neighborhoods – racially and ethnically mixed as possible."

These words and similar statements most likely influenced the province's decision to move the novitiate to a working-class neighborhood in Cambridge, Massachusetts; the decision to open Duchesne House for volunteers helping to rebuild New Orleans after Hurricane Katrina; and the purchase of a building for an RSCJ community on 118th Street in East Harlem, New York City. Decisions to live in diverse neighborhoods also introduced wider groups of women to the Society. As Irma Dillard, RSCJ, wrote, when asked to share her memories for this book,

> I met RSCJ in the summer of 1969, my junior year in high school. They had just left the big house, what was then called Convent of the Sacred Heart, Menlo Park, [California] to begin a new ministry in Saint Francis of Assisi Parish in East Palo Alto. I was walking my little sister to the summer program at the church, when Mother Marie McHugh, who wore a modified habit, greeted me. She asked me what I was doing for the summer. I was already very involved in the parish and could not tell this nun 'no' to her invitation to work in the summer program.

Sister Dillard joined the Society in 1974 and remains among the members active in works for justice.

Melanie Guste, RSCJ, reflecting on the source of her own vocation while a student at the Academy of the Sacred Heart in New Orleans, wrote in comments for this book:

> The same Spirit that led these RSCJ from living and working in schools to direct service with the poor and to work for justice, led me to discern my vocational call to the Religious of the Sacred Heart. I saw these sisters as faithful to the call of the Church at the time, and making radical personal choices with integrity and courage.

Internationality

Introduction

The seeds of internationality were planted in the Society of the Sacred from its earliest days. Madeleine Sophie Barat longed to make the love of the Heart of Jesus known beyond the borders of her native France; and in 1818, just eighteen years after the founding of the Society, Philippine Duchesne and four companions set sail for America. They were the first in a long line of women who lived their mission as RSCJ in countries other than their own. Theirs were the first steps of the Society in its growth as an international congregation.

Traditionally, men and women who went abroad as Christian missionaries did so with a desire to bring the gospel to those to whom it had not yet been announced. Before the Second Vatican Council, many RSCJ went to other countries for this purpose. But, as had been the case for Philippine Duchesne, their horizons were soon stretched. Activities in the areas of human development, such as education and health care, became ways of living the gospel, and the Second Vatican Council made this perspective explicit in the field of mission. Previously, to be "sent" had meant, in most instances, to go to peoples who had little access to the modern benefits of science, education, and development. After the council, the goal was to become "good news" for others: "The joys and the hopes, the griefs and the anxieties of the men of this age, especially those who are poor or in any way afflicted, these are the joys and hopes, the griefs and anxieties of the followers of Christ. Indeed, nothing genuinely human fails to raise an echo in their hearts."[87] Justice and peace, and in later years, care for our common home, became intrinsic dimensions of mission.

This chapter presents the memories and reflections of several RSCJ who, having lived their religious commitment in countries other than their own, bear witness to internationality as a call heard, a challenge lived, and a gift received.

Responding to the Call

For Helen O'Regan, RSCJ, the call to serve in a developing country was linked intimately with the call to fulfill the Society's commitment to internationality:

> While teaching at Nottingham Academy of the Sacred Heart in Buffalo, New York, I was asked if I wanted to become certified as a teacher or go into nursing. I chose the latter. Halfway through the training, I felt a call to serve in a developing country. The value of community life and serving the poor as a nurse did not seem possible in the United States, but it looked very

> possible in other countries where the Society [was established.] I imagined a community serving … with a variety of skills.

Sister O'Regan went on to serve as a nurse and educator in Kenya for over twenty years, helping people to understand and address the AIDS epidemic in the Diocese of Eldoret and elsewhere.

The call Carol Bialock, RSCJ, heard to be a missionary was clear, even before meeting the RSCJ. But it took a definite turn when she learned about Philippine Duchesne.

> A friend took me to a Presbyterian retreat, where I heard a couple give testimony of their lives as missionaries in Japan. I left the hall knowing that I would be a Presbyterian missionary. My father put me in our boarding school at St. Charles, Missouri—the Academy of the Sacred Heart—when I was fifteen. Philippine Duchesne's missionary zeal won me to the Catholic Church and at the same time renewed my missionary vocation.

Gwendolyn (Gwen) Hoeffel, RSCJ, describes the attraction to experience internationality, first as a lay missionary volunteer. She graduated from the Society's Manhattanville College in 1964 with a strong sense of gratitude to Sister Brigid Keogh, provincial in the Far East, who had opened the first RSCJ community in Korea in 1956. "Sister Keogh was very supportive of the Society's missionary volunteer program that I read about in the little magazine *Mitte Me,*" Sister Hoeffel said. "She actively accepted young women to come to the Far East Province." That province included Japan, Korea, Taiwan, and the Philippines. Sister Hoeffel taught for a year in the Sacred Heart International School in Tokyo, an experience that opened another door and presented a new opportunity. "During my first year as a missionary volunteer, I realized that English was one of the languages used in the RSCJ noviceship. I decided to ask that fall if I could enter the noviceship and be a missionary from the start."

In the 1970's the Society of the Sacred Heart began inviting religious who had been professed for many decades to come to Rome for a time of renewal, which was called *recyclage*. This period of renewal opened new vistas to Rosemary (Rosie) Statt, RSCJ:

> My call to the Uganda/Kenya Province originated there. After spending six months in the (Uganda/Kenya) Province as part of my year of *recyclage* in 1975-76, I could not get that province's needs, its spirit, nor my call for the poor out of my heart. While I worked in the inner city of New York for three years, my heart kept pulling me back to East Africa. I gave in.

Years later, she still felt "that inside me is a very beautiful gem: my ten years in East Africa. How often I gaze on it in wonder and in prayer. How dearly I miss the internationality I so love and which was so tangible in East Africa." Sister Statt returned to Africa in 1979 and spent ten more years serving in Uganda.

Dolores (Lolin) Menéndez, RSCJ, felt drawn to Africa too, and an experience in Uganda soon after her arrival made clear to her what lay at the heart of her call.

> A casual conversation brought home to me a difference in perspective. In the late 1970s, after living for a year or two in Karamoja, a far-off and underdeveloped region of Uganda, an Italian sister of a missionary congregation said to me: "I admire you Religious of the Sacred Heart for coming to this remote area of tremendous hardships and staying. After all, you are not a missionary congregation." Politely, (I hope) I pointed out that before their founder was born, five RSCJ had crossed the Atlantic to the North American "missions," and that by 1842 we had a house in Algiers. "Yes," I continued, "we are not a missionary congregation as such. But we are an international congregation, faithful to the mission of making known the love of the Heart of Jesus through the service of education, wherever we are sent." I had not given much thought to "mission versus internationality" before going to Africa, but from that day onward, internationality became the leitmotif of my service.

Without doubt, living in a context different from one's own presented challenges that the RSCJ learned to live with, if not overcome. The first step was to consciously put aside intellectual, spiritual and personal baggage. This did not happen at once; it was essential to keep asking questions, to learn to live with one's questions, and to let oneself be challenged and changed by the answers.

Concepción (Concha) Camacho, RSCJ, after becoming the Society's superior general at the Chapter of 1970, closed the chapter with these words: "The most difficult renunciation we can make is that of our own culture. This kind of renunciation we must make; we must live in international understanding, eager to learn from others and to be mutually helpful." These words made a deep impact on Constance (Connie) Dryden, RSCJ, who spent most of the 1980s in the Uganda/Kenya Province. She wrote: "When I arrived in Kenya hoping to join that province, I realized I had to rethink everything I thought I knew, about everything! I had to accept ways of being and doing that were different, but no less valid, from the ways I had assumed for many years to be the right ones."

Margaret Mary (Mike) Hoffman, RSCJ, also questioned her past assumptions:

> I was sent to the northeast area of Uganda to work with a health team that went to set up a mobile treatment clinic near villages of the Karimojong tribe. I found myself listening intently to these beautiful people, whose life style is so different from what I had been used to. I found them to be such rich, strong and proud people. I wondered and reflected on what I was really here for. Was I doing them more harm by bringing my Western ideas and values? What message of Christ was I speaking to them by my life?

Beatrice Brennan, RSCJ, in Egypt, pondered the need for a dialogue of cultures, the need to discern and not to judge, and then perhaps to act: "What was cluttering (that) space were the 'oughts' I had carried with me from the past. Instead of accepting what is, I kept imposing on it my idea of what should be."

Internationality did not happen without pain, nor was every international venture successful. As Mary Catherine McKay, RSCJ, reflected on her experience in Nicaragua, she lamented: "We were an international community in Jalapa and we did not do very well at this.... We were pushed to the extreme and we were found wanting," she acknowledged with humility. The community in Nicaragua was in the middle of a war-zone and faced terrible realities and eventually closed.[88]

Serving with the Heart of an Educator

Whatever mode the presence of the RSCJ takes in any country, in whatever field she is active, the ministry is always marked by an educational dimension; that is, being present with "the heart of an educator," meeting the challenge to do more than teach; to recognize and bring out the riches in each person, under the impulse of the love of the Heart of Jesus. "To Educate is in itself an act of justice," wrote The General Council, for the Feast of the Sacred Heart in 2006. The activities of RSCJ who went abroad were already framed in this perspective. Sister O'Regan reflected realistically on what it means to be an educator and an RSCJ:

> The nursing profession broadened my understanding of education. I understood from the 1970 Chapter that however we served, there was a call to be educative about it. For instance, in Karamoja being educative might mean teaching young mothers how tetanus was transmitted at birth and to have the midwife pass the spear (for a boy) or knife (for a girl) through fire before using it to cut the umbilical cord. I had to do this through my bi-lingual assistant.

In dispensaries and clinics, it was not just a question of curing, but of educating for life. This became poignantly clear during the AIDS crisis. There was careful planning of a health curriculum as well as the training of the assistants with whom the RSCJ worked.

Sister McKay was very clear about the educational dimension as well. "In Nicaragua I also learned something more about being an educator according to the mind of Madeleine Sophie and the Heart of Jesus .... We accompanied many groups as they discovered resources within themselves and put them at the service of the transformation of society."

Sister Menéndez, after several years teaching in Saced Heart schools— Stone Ridge in Bethesda, Maryland, and Carrollton in Miami—saw for herself that there were many who longed for the kind of education offered in schools run by the Society, yet had no access to it. The call to share what she had experienced and learned led her to Uganda, first to a teacher training college, then to parishes for the formation of catechists, leaders and women, eventually to many years of involvement in the development of educational programs in refugee camps throughout Africa and Asia. She reflected:

> Those who offered to serve abroad went with a conviction that ours was a secondary, supporting role, and this disposition would enflesh our "passion to proclaim the Gospel" in creative ways. Training local teachers meant putting aside the joys of teaching children ourselves in favor of enabling others to be formed in methodology and content so that they would teach their own younger generations. If we had come with more and different skills, it was in order to put them at the service of those to whom we were sent. I am sure it is what Madeleine Sophie wanted!

Sister Brennan spoke about finding the delicate balance between respect for a way of life and the challenge of opening possibilities that are new or different,—perhaps encouraging people to take a step away from their tradition in the interest of improving their wellbeing. She began questioning her own judgments about life in other contexts, and wondering whether they might be unjust.

> I might question why children run dirty and unkempt in the streets, but most village mothers, who are almost always pregnant or nursing a baby, must carry water some distance from a public faucet. In their place, how would I manage with children? But does accepting the way things are mean that we should do nothing to make it better? Being in touch with the lives of women has helped us to discover how concretely the Lord wants us to "seek justice with the heart of an educator." The best we can offer is our friendship in times of sorrow and joy, of sharing what we have. And of learning from them the simple wisdom and faith that gives such beauty to their lives.

Cross-Cultural Exchange

Inevitably, RSCJ were enriched by new, cross-cultural friendships, friendships that entailed receiving as well as giving. RSCJ who served in other countries during this period became keenly aware that lessons learned and gifts received went beyond what they had imagined. In many cases, this transformation happened gradually, but it became a central dimension and a treasured part of international service for those who served abroad.

Sister Hoffman, in a letter she wrote in 1989, reflected on her time living among the Karamajong people in the Uganda/Kenya Province: "I felt very strongly about the need to receive from the people I helped as well as giving of myself," and she came to regard herself as a listener and facilitator. "I learned to listen closely to the people I worked with, to be present to their needs, and especially to hear their own solutions to their problems."

Sister Menéndez summed up her twenty-seven years in Africa this way: "We received new lessons about interpersonal relationships; for example, that persons come first, ahead of concerns about being on time. Ï repeat, many years afterwards, that Africa has mentored me."

Muriel Cameron, RSCJ, experienced the gift of internationality in her life abroad, not only in Japan and the Dominican Republic, but also in her work with migrant workers within the borders of her own country. She describes that work as her "university of life," from which she gained a deeper understanding of social problems. "Issues of injustice take on unforgettable human faces, and the complexities constantly unfold," she said. "But not only does one see the suffering or meanness embedded in particular situations; one also discovers that somewhere there is always radiant beauty. This beauty could be in the hope, communal love, courage, determination, and spirit of familial sacrifices or sense of joy found in the human spirit."

Sister Bialock found that her experience deepened her understanding of the gospel. "I became a Chilean citizen as a small gesture of identification with my adopted people. I began to understand the Beatitudes there. I began to learn to be a Christian there."

RSCJ spoke, too, of their experiences of interculturality. While many religious communities in the countries where RSCJ went to serve during these years drew women from similar tribes or social groups, the Society of the Sacred Heart looked for a wider understanding of community, one that could embrace differences. "Looking back from today, I see that, while maintaining our own identity, which includes our culture, we needed to embrace and enter into the culture of the other," reflected Sister Dryden. Her experience taught her the demands of interculturality, not only on the RSCJ who came to Africa from abroad, but also for the African women who entered the Society. "They joined a group that was different from some African religious congregations," she said. "We were establishing an 'intercultural' community,' and the African sisters were invited to embrace our values and practices, just as we were expected to embrace and value theirs," she said. "This meant they had to have more than an international viewpoint. They had to live interculturality, truly."

Reflecting on the years she lived in Japan, Sister Hoeffel pointed to a new opportunity offered to her when she worked with immigrants and refugees in Nagoya:

> Working with non-Japanese people in homogeneous Japan, I was in a multicultural population that needed bridge builders in order for people not only to live together but also to grow to understand and accept one another, and to ensure the continuing transformation of the Church in Japan into a more universal church. I understood that I could be a bridge for these foreigners into Japanese culture. I had lived in Japan for fifty years. I could speak the language. I too was a foreigner there, I knew some of the dynamics, so I could be their voice and advocate.

Sister O'Regan came to realize that developing human relationships required attempting to learn the other person's language. She also realized that just as there is no one American culture, there is no one African culture. In living out internationality in 1975 in Karamoja, Uganda, and in Chekalini, Kenya, "I became aware of our Cor Unum with RSCJ from many countries," Sister O'Regan said.

A Different Experience of Church

During their international service, RSCJ were called to be church in different ways, to be part of a young church, of a church where the winds of change were beginning to blow.

Sister Bialock writes of her joy when she first set foot on Chilean soil:

> I knew this was the place for me. The Latin American bishops had just returned from the Medellín Conference that implemented Vatican II for South and Central America. The poor were to be given priority, and it was precisely for the poor that I had come. The bishops of Chile had asked religious to respond by going to the poor, and the Society of the Sacred Heart was one of the first to respond.

During her years in Japan, Sister Hoeffel was very much a part of the local church. Different moments offered her different experiences. She speaks about her time in the novitiate at Susono, in the late 1960s: "Soon the documents from the Second Vatican Council became our reading material, and well informed Jesuits were invited to give talks. My mind expanded in so many ways, including what being a missionary meant. It was not difficult to recognize the Spirit at work in Japanese culture, in the hearts of the people. The challenge of becoming the church in Japan and not simply a Japanese church is an ongoing endeavor."

Years later, Sister Hoffel experienced a different facet of the life of the Catholic Church in Japan:

> In order to follow the call of the council to return to the charism of our foundress, which Sister Keogh knew included reaching out to the marginalized, she accepted the invitation from Reverend Thomas Purcell, OSA, to start a community in Nagoya among the Catholic immigrants from Nagasaki, who had come to this industrial city for work—the dirty, dangerous, difficult kind of work. Sister Keogh knew of my desire to be part of a ministry among the less privileged people in Japan, the invisible and unknown people. I was one of the fortunate sisters to start this new endeavor.

Sister O'Regan underlines the aspects of being part of the local church that she appreciated during her years in Africa:

> The sense of church as a community with human bonds as we served together: RSCJ from different provinces, sisters, priests and brothers from different congregations. The bishops were near their people. The Eucharist was central to celebrations. Relating and collaborating as church with one mission was a significant strength." For some, this was a very different reality from the church they had experienced in their country of origin, and they said they treasured it as one of the gifts received.

Witness to Sisterhood and Brotherhood in Christ

The presence of RSCJ in international communities gave an explicit witness to the sisterhood and brotherhood to which all Christians are called. The province of Uganda/Kenya was an international foundation from its first days. A few years later, there were RSCJ from five continents serving in both countries, and it was not unusual to have more than four nationalities present in a community, as well as sisters from different indigenous tribes. It was a microcosm of the universal church. Sister Menéndez remembers: "A conversation with an official at an immigration post on the border of Uganda and Kenya brought this home: 'What? Five passports from five different countries and you all live at the same address?' 'Yes, we live together.' 'Five different tribes? Can you all live together without fighting?' This made our community realize that our living internationality is a gospel witness that the Society brings to the Church."

When It Is Time to Leave

The decision to stay or to return, framed in discernment, is a component of the call to serve in another country. For some RSCJ, a time comes when it is right to return to one's country, transformed by life experiences, bearing unexpected gifts. Before the Second Vatican Council, many RSCJ who went abroad stayed there until death. We think of Philippine Duchesne, Anna du Rousier, and in our own time, Brigid Keogh. Many others who find it better to return and spend their final years in their native country still find it difficult to leave their adopted countries behind.

"I returned to the States three years ago," said Sister Bialock. "I am still adjusting. I do not want total adjustment. I do not want to forget what Chile taught me."

An Italian priest told Sister Menéndez on the drive to the airport for her first home leave: "Today you are happy because you are going home. In a month, you will think of Africa. In two, you will be homesick for Africa. And in three, you will count the days until you return. Once Africa gets in your blood, it will never leave you." Many RSCJ who have lived in Africa would say it's true.

Sister Hoeffel discerned that she would return permanently to the United States in 2014. She writes:

> Since I entered in Japan I belonged to and identified with life in Japan and the lives of our sisters in the Japanese Province. I thought mostly that I would bury my bones in Japan. But a time came that I felt called to discern more openly and freely whether to stay into old age or return to the USA and our USC province before I became too old to adapt. Obviously, returning to my home roots won, but Japan is still very much part of me. I have no regrets, just immense gratitude and the desire to truly live the reality of being one body.

For some RSCJ staying means fidelity to a process, to a people. Sister Hoffman underlines an experience common to many RSCJ:

> Another consideration I have come to realize about my staying in East Africa is that our congregation is becoming indigenous and that these young RSCJ need to be heard and supported toward the time when the province will become self-directed. Along with this, I have gained so much by my life here, by this rich experience, and now I am able to praise and thank God that I had the opportunity to go to East Africa.

Sister O'Regan added that there was a need for finally professed RSCJ to accompany the East Africans who were entering as candidates. "I felt I could contribute here," she said, recalling the words of the Society's *Constitutions*: "The fate of the Society is in our hands."

During a visit to the RSCJ community in Haiti, Diane Roche, RSCJ, had a conversation that sums up the present understanding and practice of internationality and mission.

> On the last day of my visit, I asked two of the sisters to tell me in their own words what is at the heart of the work they do in the school, what keeps them motivated despite the challenges; for example, getting robbed by armed men just outside the school. It is exactly the depth of the discouragement and frustration in Haiti that motivates the RSCJ to stay and continue the work. They see that the main need in Haiti (and in many of the other places in which they have served over the years) is human development, and that includes making the connection between helping people to recognize their own worth and the good news of the gospel.

Conclusion: Beyond internationality

In 1982, the Society of the Sacred Heart embarked on examination of the *Constitutions* of 1815 in order to express their essence in contemporary terms. At the heart of the revised *Constitutions* remains the call to communicate the love of the Heart of Jesus by the way that Religious of the Sacred Heart live the gospel.

Internationality is a way of extending the mission; but neither the *Constitutions* nor the path travelled in the last fifty years after Vatican II mark a final stage in the understanding of internationality for the Society of the Sacred Heart. The Society's understanding is stretched by new insights and calls coming from the world and from the Church.

A few quotes from the Society's recent chapter documents indicate further steps: From General Chapter 1988: "We began to understand in a new way that inculturation is shaping our way of being, our way of serving the people of God and our understanding of internationality."

From General Chapter 1994:

> We are convinced that our living internationality is no longer a choice but a responsibility in the face of the calls of today. The extent of our internationality, which is rooted in our charism, calls us more and more to respond to the needs of the world, especially to the powerless and marginalized.

From General Chapter 2016:

> To go out, to 'set sail' as a Society and go with others to new geographic and existential peripheries to accompany the life that is emerging there, to defend justice, peace, and the integrity of creation in response to all of those who are searching for meaning in their lives, those who have been wounded, displaced, and excluded because of poverty, violence, and environmental degradation.

There is a quote often attributed to Saint Madeleine Sophie that says, "Within the Sacred Heart you have no country but the whole universe." While it is not certain that these words are from Sophie's own pen, they do highlight the reality that internationality is integral to the Society's self-understanding. It is, indeed, the Society's journey.

Working for Systemic Change & Human Rights

In the course of history, there comes a time when humanity is called to shift to a new level of consciousness, to reach a higher moral ground. A time when we have to shed our fear and give hope to each other. That time is now.[89]

– Wangari Maathai

Introduction

For decades, the need to address inequalities and disparities in our contemporary world has driven religious women and men, including Religious of the Sacred Heart, to undertake advocacy efforts aimed at systemic social change. Motivated by the gospel, inspired by Catholic social thought, and basing their advocacy on what they have seen and experienced by living with marginalized people, members of faith-based organizations and groups have exposed countless areas of systemic imbalances rooted in discrimination. Many RSCJ, whose mission it is to discover and reveal the love of Christ's heart in the very heart of the world, have responded to the need to right these wrongs as "a call within a call."

This chapter explores how and why some RSCJ took courageous stands against dehumanizing inequality and marginalization in areas such as housing, welfare, immigration, and worker's rights, while others put themselves wholeheartedly into national and international peace efforts, anti-war actions, acts of nonviolence and civil rights. They were extraordinary trailblazers who were willing to change themselves and take personal risks in the interest of bettering lives and bringing justice and peace to a troubled world. The chapter also briefly examines how the Society of the Sacred Heart in the United States pursued justice within its own structures, in particular through choices made in each province's finance office.[90]

Motivations

What impelled these women to change their religious habits for simple dress, even jeans, and go out to society's peripheries? Undoubtedly, their life of prayer invited them to articulate in deeds their conviction that a more just world was possible. As educators, even if cloistered, they knew of the disparities between people with financial resources that allowed them to make educational choices for their children, and those without. Moreover, the 1960s were uncertain and even turbulent times in general, both politically and militarily, resulting from decolonization in, for example, Africa and Southeast Asia, the ongoing Cold War between the United States and the USSR, and movements aimed at addressing discrimination and disparities at home. From an ecclesial perspective, it was the time when small groups of Christians, so-called Christian base communities, began to develop, mainly in Latin America, as outgrowths of liberation theology. These are small groups, based on gospel values, in which the participation of the vulnerable themselves is critical to the focus on liberation from political, social and economic oppression. Having followed these movements, and prayed with the words and attitudes of Jesus, many RSCJ had a deep desire to follow Christ more closely by practicing gospel values such as nonviolence, solidarity with the crucified and forgotten, and the defense of each person's human dignity as a child of God. These women firmly believed in their co-responsibility. In the words of a key Society document that was published just months before the 1988 General Chapter, the "God in whom we profess belief is a God who engages us in making all things new" and who calls us to "be co-creators of life and energy, of new connections and new configurations."[91]

Although in many faith-based circles the widespread sentiment still existed that priests and nuns should keep to the gospel and not mix in politics, the 1988 General Chapter would go on to explicitly address the political dimension of the Society's mission. Yet for those RSCJ who would make radical choices to address society's ills, some tough choices lay ahead.

Politics and Housing Rights

For two RSCJ, Katherine McDonnell and Joan Kirby, it was clear well before 1988 that gospel values and politics reinforce each other and are not as separate as many people believe, especially as they relate to fundamentals such as human equality and solidarity, and the dignity of persons living in poverty,

In 1969, Sister McDonnell, encouraged by her cousin, Father Horace McKenna, SJ, a noted advocate for the marginalized, was one of six RSCJ pioneers to move into *Sursum Corda*, a low-income housing complex in Washington, D.C.[92] Of her time living in *Sursum Corda*, Sister McDonnell said, "Reflection became a daily reality around the issues of housing, health, wages, job skills, family stability and education for our new community. Our ministries grew out of the insights we gleaned here, living among families at risk. Our commitment to our neighbors brought us in touch with most issues of their lives."[93]

Sister McDonnell was clearly presented as a woman with a mission in a *Washington Post* article describing her journey as a housing advocate:

> In 1972, she submitted a proposal to the Department of Housing and Urban Development for a program to train housing professionals in counseling. Within a few days, she received a grant that enabled her to open Housing Counseling Services at 2436 18th Street, NW. It became one of the city's most influential housing agencies, negotiating with landlords and creditors, helping poor renters convert rental buildings to cooperatives and condominiums, and assisting new home owners.[94]

One of Sister McDonnell's RSCJ sisters described her as "a special person, on fire to help the poor get their rights and some decent housing.... She was a little powerhouse who was not afraid to take on power where little folks were feeling oppression."[95]

During a gala celebration in 1987, to commemorate the fifteenth anniversary of NETWORK, the Catholic Social Justice Lobby. Sister McDonnell received the Clare Dunn, CSJ, Award in recognition of her sixteen years of direct service to and housing advocacy on behalf of numerous destitute families. The plaque reads:[96]

> To Kate McDonnell, RSCJ, who continues to live out Clare Dunn's belief that politics is a way to "witness to God's care for the least of our brothers and sisters, God's concern for the marginal and powerless."

Thus, Sister McDonnell demonstrated the deep interconnectedness between listening, direct service, and advocacy.[97]

Two more RSCJ must be mentioned in this context. As so many RSCJ had done before her, Sister Kirby made a radical shift towards the grass roots following many years of ministry in formal education as a teacher and as headmistress at 91st Street in New York. Living in Hell's Kitchen in New York City, she served in the early 1980s as a housing counselor and director of home ownership for the Housing Conservation Coordinators, a neighborhood-based, not-for-profit organization dedicated to helping low-income people with housing needs. Subsequently she served as executive director and president of Homes for the Homeless in New York, a public-private organization formed in 1986 to address issues of homelessness, and as a member of the city's Community Planning Board, which advised government agencies and elected officials on matters related to social welfare in their districts.[98] Trained in philosophy, Sister Kirby was both an educator and policy worker who was deeply at home in interreligious dialogue. Her unique combination of gifts contributed to her strong ability to think systemically, which came to full bloom later, during her years at the Temple of Understanding.

The second who needs mentioning is Margaret Smith, RSCJ, who, along with Sisters Kate McDonnell and Alice McDonell, was among the forty-seven Catholic sisters who, in 1971, founded NETWORK, the social justice lobby that conferred the Clare Dunn award on Sister Kate McDonnell. Sister Smith's work for justice in Rochester, New York, included working for structural changes to eliminate poverty and racism and protesting nuclear weapons, for which she was arrested. However, her most intense activism was around the role of women in the Catholic Church. She attended the first Women's Ordination Conference in 1975, and she worked with the Women's Ordination Conference offices in Rochester and in Vienna, Virginia, becoming a member of its leadership team.

Welfare Recipients are with Rights

Margaret Mary Power, RSCJ, was a warm, intelligent and forward-thinking Canadian who ministered in Sacred Heart schools in Canada and the United States until her retirement in 1973. After a lifetime spent in school administration, while teaching Catholic social thought on the side, retirement enabled her to serve people living in poverty in a new and more radical way.

Being fully bilingual in English and French and a ferocious reader, Sister Power began her second calling by moving with two other RSCJ to Little Burgundy in Montreal, a neighborhood of mostly illiterate and defenseless persons. She said of her early days in Little Burgundy:

> I took a course with the "*avocats populaires*" on Bill 26. It was the law, which came out in 1969, that gave welfare people the right to a subsistence. They asked me to work with them and so things came together. I also read a good deal about Liberation Theology and felt that, though God is everywhere, he is particularly where the poor are, and I wanted to be where God was.[99]

Influenced by both Liberation Theology and Paulo Freire and his philosophy of popular education,[100] Sister Power began investigating the systemic root causes of poverty she encountered. She sought to learn why some people were poor and vulnerable and how was it that they could be trampled upon by municipal authorities, having water or utilities cut off, for example, without the tools to defend themselves. Her eyes were on the local government where systemic change was necessary. Reflecting on how she had been working with well-to-do people in Sacred Heart schools, she said,

"I used to encourage giving to charity … but I never said that we have to change the world and not have all these poor people." What I teach now is that we've got to change the world so these people don't need our handouts. What bothers me is not individual selfishness but the structures that are in place which exploit people.[101]

Sister Power, a delegate to the Society's General Chapter of 1970, felt affirmed in her work when the chapter declared its support for solidarity with the poor and the oppressed in developing nations. Identifying herself with the oppressed and forgotten in Little Burgundy, a low-income neighborhood in Montreal, she founded *Organisation d'aide aux Assistés Sociaux;* and, being the educator she was, she described its objectives as follows: "Our aim is to help welfare people run their own lives. We teach welfare recipients the law and what their rights are.… What we try to do is make them realize that they have a right to a job, a right to respect, a right to be heard and listened to like anybody else. They are 'inferiorized' by all kinds of experiences."[102]

Looking back on her life in service to the powerless in Little Burgundy, she summarized her mission, "I'm a nun because I was seeking God in an absolute kind of way.... I want to be doing something that will help to liberate people on whatever level I can."[103]

In other words, for Sister Power working towards systemic change and providing direct service had to go together in order to be effective. Today an approach that is inclusive of multiple stakeholders, including the vulnerable themselves, is a bedrock principle of evidence-based advocacy for systemic change.

Solidarity with Farmworkers

From the early 1960s and into the 1980s, many RSCJ heard the call to serve migrant farmworkers in their quest for justice. It was the time of the grape boycotts and strikes aimed at improving conditions for grape workers, the time of labor leader Cesar Chavez's activism and his founding of the United Farm Workers Union. At first, RSCJ devoted their energies to listening and providing direct service to people, not necessarily directly advocating for changes in the law. Yet their ministry often grew into one of seeking systemic change through their bottom-up approach.

The farmworkers' plight was quite familiar to Catholic social justice advocates. The journey of Mary (Be) Mardel and Carol Naumann, both RSCJ, to stand with the marginalized began with the United Farm Workers strike in the mid-1960s in California. Then came 1973, and Sister Naumann and Sister Mardel, who had begun her tenure as provincial of the former San Francisco Province in 1972, joined the farmworkers in their protest, were arrested, and spent two weeks in jail. Here is the story.[104]

Farmworkers were demonstrating in Fresno, California, despite an injunction against assembling, and they invited others to march with them. Sister Mardel felt a deep call to put her solidarity into action, knowing that the Catholic bishops had just released a statement supporting the farmworkers, as had superiors of some major congregations of women and men religious. Sister Mardel was ready for courageous action to make the Church's support of the farmworkers visible. Many demonstrators were arrested and jailed for what was initially expected to be an overnight, but the authorities decided otherwise. When San Francisco Mayor and Sacred Heart alumna Dianne Feinstein, later a US Senator from California, heard about Sister Mardel's incarceration, she called her on the phone, exclaiming, "Mother Mardel, what are YOU doing in jail?" Miles away, upon learning that nuns and priests had been detained, Catholic social activist Dorothy Day and a group of sisters from the East Coast soon joined the protesters in California. They too were arrested, and Dorothy Day was jailed in the barracks next to Sister Mardel.

In a letter to her province, dated August 10, 1973, in which she recounts daily struggles in prison and its profound effect on her spiritual life, Sister Mardel wrote:

> Trudy[105] was also able to get Mr. Mayo Mohs, religion editor of *Time*, New York, to call me, and he intends to do a story on the problem. He is very sympathetic to the cause of the farmworkers. "You're doing just what the bishops are telling us to do," he said, and was interested to know that Dorothy Day was here (What an inspiration that old lady is to all of us!) [and] that Bishops Metzger from El Paso and Arzube from Los Angeles, with eight priests, said Mass for the 150 of us in the "yard" (a lovely lawn all around our dorms, surrounded by high cyclone fence, barbed wire and padlocked gates). Dorothy Day says she does not think sixty-two priests and nuns have ever been arrested at one time in one place for the same cause before. She is delighted, of course.

In that same letter, Sister Mardel writes that she finds the experience in jail quite "inexpressible!… a revelation of another world at our doorstep, where beautiful, loving, warm, generous, courageous people have *so* little power, are so put down and know so little about what to do to remedy the pain of their lives."

In another document, Sister Mardel describes this time in jail as "my first experience of feeling ONE with my suffering, poor and unjustly-treated brothers and sisters …."[106] Her days in jail were truly a time of deep grace and profound transformation. In the letter to her province, Sister Mardel wrote:

> I'm seeing life really lived in common here, where all is shared. We nuns have shared our telegrams and letters for mutual support and many—in fact, all but two—have received great encouragement and support in their stand from those in authority: Srs. Margaret Brennan and Ethne Kennedy, Network, Sumore, and many other groups, too, see the urgency of struggle for the rights of the 1st Amendment, whether one goes along with Chavez or not. The cause is MUCH bigger than the UFW or the Teamsters, and we're realizing this more every day we're here.

Acting upon the call to solidarity expressed by the Society's General Chapter 1970, Sister Mardel resolved to take a strong and uncompromising stand in union with the farmworkers. When release was offered to the women and men religious, they collectively declined unless the farmworkers would be released at the same time. In her 2020 letter for the Feast of the Sacred Heart, Superior General Sister Barbara Dawson reiterated the call to stand with the poor in their suffering: "Enter into the pierced heart of Jesus, experience the suffering of God's people and all creation, be in solidarity with each other and with people who are suffering, do not sit and wait, discover anew the ways for our time to manifest God's love."[107]

Around the same time, Mary Dowling, RSCJ, brought a different twist to this mission. A story goes that Sister Dowling went "to as many grocery stores in the

St. Louis area as possible in order to promote the Cesar Chavez grape boycott. Since she didn't drive, she enlisted former students and parents to accompany her on these excursions, thus greatly expanding consciousness of the issues."[108]

The Crucified of Our Time: Refugees and Migrants

In the late 1970s and throughout most of the 1980s, Central America was a volatile region, with civil wars and revolutions in El Salvador, Guatemala, and Nicaragua. Major socioeconomic changes had resulted in severe oppression and persecution of the largely poor populations, causing them to flee their home countries in search of safety and protection. Thus, a wave of refugees began its trek to the north, *El Norte*—the United States.

Recognizing the utter vulnerability of these Central American dispossessed as new signs of the times, many RSCJ responded with pastoral care and accompaniment, community services, or legal services and advocacy. Frances Tobin, RSCJ, upon completion of her law degree in 1983, litigated many deportation cases while serving at the Central America Refugee Center in Houston, and at Catholic Charities Immigration Services in San Diego. When asked what stands out about her wide experience as an immigration lawyer, Sister Tobin recently said that it is impossible to do immigration work "without realizing that there is a lot of racial stuff in there. Racism has existed in this country for a very long time."[109]

At the request of then-ministry director Sister Barbara Dawson, Suzanne Lasseigne, RSCJ, began her service at the Immigration Detention Center in Oakdale, Louisiana, in 1986. Sister Lasseigne remembers that time:

> In 1986 Barb asked me to go to Oakdale, Louisiana, to minister in a new Immigration Detention Center. The government had just opened it as a fully equipped deportation processing (landings strips and helipads, judges, etc.) center for Central Americans crossing the border with Mexico. This was at the height of the wars in Nicaragua and El Salvador. We spent many hours hearing the same/similar stories from civilians being tortured or threatened if they did not fight on one side or the other. I had no answers. Many RSCJ communities sent bond money for people to join their families in the United States. Eventually, the U.S. government scattered the Central Americans to jails all over Louisiana and put Cubans there.[110]

Sister Lasseigne looks back at this period in her life as highly emotional and profoundly transformative. "Jesus Christ was in all those stories.[111] Most were *campesinos* or catechists, and although they came from different countries or from diverse regions within a certain country, their stories were shockingly similar as they described the oppression, violence and persecution. 'How could anyone not believe these refugees if each one said the same thing but they came from different corners of Central America'?"[112]

Margaret Phelan, RSCJ, began her ministry on behalf of refugees as a part-time volunteer in the Refugee Resettlement Office of Catholic Charities of San Francisco in 1980. Her initial assignment was to process the paperwork submitted from within refugee camps by applicants for refugee status coming from all over the world except from Southeast Asia. She would also verify the person's sponsorship through either a parish or an immediate family member. She remembers the cases of family reunification as particularly gratifying.

That Sister Phelan was not working on actual cases involving refugees from Southeast Asia, in particular Cambodia, Vietnam and Laos, had a practical reason: she did not have those languages in her wide array of language skills. But she was fluent in Spanish, and that landed the resettlement cases of the Mariel Cubans on her desk.[113] During the chaos of the Mariel Boatlift, Sister Phelan would frequently connect with her contacts at the refugee camp set up at Fort Smith, Arkansas, while also connecting with the leaders of the Cuban community in the San Francisco Bay Area, trying to find sponsors and places to house the mostly single male refugees. With transparency lacking, however, criminal actions by some of these sponsors and leaders were endangering the refugees, leaving the latter vulnerable to exploitation and dangers of many sorts—a gloomy example of corruption that is not uncommon in refugee situations, even today.

Meanwhile Sister Phelan also received training in immigration law and became qualified and certified as a legal representative before the former Immigration and Naturalization Service (INS)[114] and the immigration court. Most of the people she worked with were migrant farmworkers who had been picked up during INS raids for lack of proper documents.

In 1984, Sister Phelan began working with Catholic Charities in Los Angeles to develop the immigration education program in the parishes of the Los Angeles archdiocese. The purpose of this program was to educate the largely undocumented Hispanic population about their rights and responsibilities. She also re-certified as a legal representative before the immigration court in Los Angeles. With the passage of the 1986 Immigration Reform and Control Act (IRCA), executing any of these responsibilities became quickly overwhelming, as many undocumented persons would knock on the door of Catholic Charities to find out whether they were eligible for some form of amnesty. As was the case all over the country, Sister Phelan's office was unprepared, understaffed, and underfunded, causing many staff members to leave from sheer exhaustion.

Whenever possible throughout the 1980s, Sister Barbara Dawson volunteered in immigration legal services and in the late 1980s became a fulltime immigration lawyer at Carecen in San Francisco.

We Are One Body—Marching for Civil Rights

In 1965, when change was in the air, several RSCJ and students from different Sacred Heart colleges received permission to participate in the historic voting rights march from Selma to Montgomery, Alabama. The march had been organized by Dr. Martin Luther King, Jr. and the Southern Christian Leadership Conference. Several earlier marches had turned violent but President Lyndon B. Johnson now promised to protect the marchers.

On March 21, about 3,200 people began a walk from Selma to Montgomery, protected by federal troops. Along the way, many more joined them, so that by the time they reached the state capitol at Montgomery, there were many thousands, including two RSCJ from Barat College in Lake Forest, Illinois, and two from Maryville College in St. Louis, in both cases accompanied by college students. In response to a telegram received three days prior, Manhattanville sent thirteen students. ... They were met upon their return by [RSCJ] Eleanor O'Byrne and Elizabeth Cavanagh.[115]

The two RSCJ from Maryville College were Anne Webster, academic dean, and Patricia Barrett, professor of political science. When interviewed at the time by *The Gong*, the Maryville student newspaper, Sister Barrett reflected "I went ... in order to give personal and public witness to my belief in the dignity of man and the unity of the human race. I saw it as an opportunity to demonstrate, as well as declare, my commitment to a social order founded on truth, justice, love and freedom."[116] Years later, Sister Barrett recalled,

> I can say, in summary, that my work with the poor had its roots in a youthful attraction to the "under-dog" (read marginalized). I simply took advantage of the opportunities that presented themselves without much thought of changing the system. I did what I could to help those in need without alienating the powers that be. The strongest expression of sympathy with the poor blacks took place in the Selma-Montgomery March in 1965. Thousands of people from all over the United States and Canada poured into Montgomery, Alabama, on the morning of March 25th where they linked up with the smaller, original group which had made the trek from Selma. The entire group gathered at the mansion of Governor George Wallace and registered their protest against his segregationist policies in songs and speeches. It was for me a unique experience of what it feels to be a despised and persecuted minority.[117]

Students from Barat College in Lake Forest and Marguerite Green and Nancy Kane, both RSCJ history professors there, also set out for Alabama to participate in the Selma to Montgomery march. In her book about the history of Barat College, Martha Curry, RSCJ, describes this episode as follows:

> On March 24, twenty-four students accompanied by the chairman of the Art Department, Albert Pounian, left by train for Montgomery, and the next

> day [Sisters] Marguerite Green and Nancy Kane flew to Montgomery. Both the train and the airplane arrived in Montgomery about noon on March 25 and, therefore, the contingent from Barat did not march with Martin Luther King the whole fifty miles from Selma. They joined the march in Montgomery at a black church, the Church of St. Jude, and continued the three-plus mile march to the capitol....
>
> Of the three faculty members who participated in the events in Montgomery, only [Sister] Kane was living at the time of the author's interviews.... She remembered that all the black churches were open that day to accommodate the marchers, and she commented on the cheering they received as they progressed through the black neighborhoods. "There was a great euphoria like we were coming into the Kingdom. . . . As we got close to [the capitol], the atmosphere changed and we were really sort of scared. . . .I never felt such hatred." [Sister] Kane went on to explain that since their flight back to Chicago did not leave until the next morning, she, [Sister Green], and Professor Pounian slept on benches in St. Jude Church overnight. The students returned to Chicago by train on the evening of March 25.[118]

Since 1965, numerous RSCJ have ministered with and alongside Americans of African descent, whether in parishes, inner city schools community services, or other ministries.

Prophets Standing Up for Peace and Nonviolence

Two core values exhibited throughout the New Testament are peace and nonviolence. Once the doors of the cloister opened, several RSCJ followed Jesus on this difficult yet prophetic road and dedicated their lives to peace and nonviolence in consequential ways.

The radical journey of Anne Montgomery, RSCJ, began in Albany and Harlem, where she experienced the effects of a shrinking United States budget on the lives of poor and disenfranchised people. Allocations for education, housing, and health care decreased as the military budget expanded in order to develop more powerful nuclear bombs, as well as a huge arsenal of newer military weapons. In response, she became a member of the Plowshares Eight, which included the Jesuit Daniel Berrigan and his brother Philip, and in 1980 began to take part in their dramatic protests against United States military and social policy, each one ending in arrest and indictment, trial, sentencing, time in either jail or prison, followed by probation or parole.[119] From the initial 1980 action, which occurred at the General Electric Plant in King of Prussia, Pennsylvania, all following Plowshares actions reflected the spirit found in Isaiah's words: "They shall beat their swords into plowshares and their spears into pruning hooks. And nations will not take up swords against nations, nor will they train for war anymore" (Isa 2:4).

For Sister Montgomery, her actions for peace and nonviolence were deeply rooted in her spirituality, which she shared generously with others. According to her obituary,

> Anne never tired of explaining that peace actions must be based on continual community prayer, reflection, decision-making, and the prayerful consensus of the group in order to sustain those who had committed themselves to nonviolent civil disobedience and nuclear disarmament. She often commented that in her several times in jail or prison, she found that most women showed great care for her and others like her imprisoned with them. In addition, many were hungry for something spiritual and most understood the great disparity between the powerful and the poor and the effects this disparity had on American society. Quite often, Anne and other peace activists assisted women by starting prayer groups, Scripture study groups, and literature groups. Once out of jail or prison, she continued to teach and speak whenever she could about the danger of nuclear weapons in a world where peace was and is so fragile.

Sister Montgomery's final Plowshares action took place in 2009 with the Disarm Now Plowshares group at the naval base Kitsap-Bangor in Washington State, home to Trident submarines and more than 2,000 nuclear warheads. Together with four other peace activists—two grandmothers and two Jesuit priests—Sister Montgomery entered the base, was arrested and charged. In federal court, the judge found all five activists guilty of trespassing and damage of federal property. They all received a prison sentence. Sister Montgomery, by then eighty-hree years old, served two months in prison, then spent four months in Washington State being monitored electronically; only then was she able to return to California for one year of supervised release while living in community with her RSCJ sisters. True to her basic beliefs and commitments, she volunteered at the local Catholic Worker during this time.

In addition to engaging in nonviolent peace actions with Plowshares, Sister Montgomery was also a member of the Christian Peacemaker Teams, an ecumenical, nonviolent, anti-war group. This association took her several times to Iraq, the Israeli-occupied West Bank, and Hebron.

Her RSCJ superiors and sisters grew in their support of Sister Montgomery's thirty-plus years of full-time ministry of presence and work as a peace activist and peacemaker. A missioning statement, sent by the Society of the Sacred Heart to Anne at a time of sentencing reads, in part: We send you, Anne, on behalf of the Society of the Sacred Heart, to continue your prophetic, educational mission with courage and grace, whether within the walls of prison or without, making known the love of Jesus for our world and all people.[120]

Sister Montgomery's obituary concludes with these simple words that characterize the essence of the holy woman she was: "Fearless and calm … contemplative and a lover of the poor, Anne stood simply and strongly against that which harmed people and the earth regardless of the cost to herself."

Sister Montgomery was by no means the only RSCJ committed to courageous action for systemic change through peacemaking and civil disobedience. Margaret Mary (Mavie) Coakley, RSCJ, was a frequent participant in marches and protests during the time she lived in Washington, D.C. At one point, she told Kathleen Cox, RSCJ, that she was going to a demonstration but would not take part in the civil disobedience at the end. A few hours later came a call from the D.C. jail, asking for a few overnight necessities and a sweater. She said she had given hers to her cellmate, "a prostitute who was cold!"[121]

Anita von Wellsheim, RSCJ, was a gifted educator who had a life-altering conversion in 1972, a "new and growing awareness of a world of suffering and injustice and an understanding of the mission to bring the good news of the gospel to the poor."[122] Ten years later, she was directing the office of refugee resettlement for the Diocese of Albany, New York, which brought her in contact with Central American refugees fleeing violence and persecution. This led her to join a Witness for Peace delegation to Nicaragua, where the group was captured by the Contras, a right-wing rebel revolutionary group, while sailing in a flotilla for peace. She became a volunteer with Witness for Peace and was a member of Pax Christi USA. Going to Haiti with a Pax Christi delegation ignited her fire of love for the brave and suffering people of Haiti, a fire that was never quenched. She learned Creole and by 1996 became involved with Fonkoze, Haiti's alternative bank known for its micro lending to persons living in poverty.

Justice Through Finance

At first glance, the connection between work for justice and the Society of the Sacred Heart as an institution may not be obvious, but the finance offices of the five provinces have done their part to bring about systemic change at different levels. As Nance O'Neil, RSCJ, has explained, justice through finance—financial advocacy—was one of her responsibilities as provincial treasurer of former New York Province (1974-1982). Some financial advocacy took place at the provincial level; other actions were the result of interprovincial collaboration, even prior to the beginning of the merger that created the United States Province in 1982. The following are some examples.[123]

In 1975, the former Chicago Province, where Marina Hernandez, RSCJ, was provincial treasurer from 1974 to 1982, had formed a stewardship committee to help safeguard the Society's values in financial matters, such as socially responsible investing.[124] At the recommendation of this committee, the province joined ICCR, the Interfaith Center on Corporate Responsibility, founded in 1971. As a member organization of ICCR, the finance office received mailings with critical information about corporations in which the Society held stock, benefited from ICCR's research and advocacy strategies, and generally was able to work together with other like-minded ICCR members in bringing a value-based voice to corporations' annual meetings through shareholder advocacy. This became an important education for everyone in the province, as they were kept abreast of the what and how of this new type of advocacy. It resulted in a statement of investment priorities that reflected the Society's values.

Another project this committee undertook was investigating so-called redlining practices by banks in which RSCJ communities had their checking accounts—that is, practices that discriminated against people of color, in particular African-Americans.

As provincial treasurer of the former St. Louis Province in the late 1970s, Agnes Hoormann, RSCJ, met regularly with treasurers from other religious congregations, exploring best practices and ways to collaborate. Through the Midwest Coalition for Responsible Investment (MCRI),[125] the issue of the "Krugerrand"[126] came up, a gold coin in vogue with investors because of its gold value. What made the sale of the Krugerrand problematic was that all profits went to support the South African government, the regime that enforced apartheid. Some local banks in the St. Louis area sold the Krugerrand, prompting MCRI members to request meetings with two particular banks to educate bank officials about what the sale of the Krugerrand represented, who benefited from the proceeds, and to advocate for a stop to this abhorrent trade. They were successful with only one of the two banks.[127]

Significant collaboration also happened in the area of ethical investing. Building on the financial advocacy described above, Sisters O'Neil, Hernandez, and Elizabeth Sweeney, RSCJ, forged a new collaboration among their respective provinces. Sister Sweeney, treasurer of the Washington Province, became investment coordinator with the aim of educating the portfolio managers about the Society's values and the need for socially responsible investing. Slowly but surely, under Sister Sweeney's skillful guidance, the portfolio managers began to understand the concept and urgency of ethical investing.

These examples show that even at the institutional level it is possible to engage with the struggle for social and political change, not necessarily by demonstrating in the streets, but by the financial choices the Society is committed to make. ICCR still exists today and is a revered advocate in shareholder activism.

Conclusion

These are the stories of RSCJ who, each in her own way, have advocated for justice and for changes in unjust systems operative in the United States and beyond. Driven by the desire to meet and serve God in right relationships so that each woman, man and child can thrive and have life, these sisters have shown what expressions of the Society's charism can look like in a post-Vatican II world. Inspired by Saint Madeleine Sophie Barat's call to generosity and humility, they made their contributions to a new world they dreamed of and longed for—God's "kingdom"; but maybe they will be remembered primarily for the way in which they embodied and lived the feelings and preferences of Jesus's heart. Reading the signs of the times that beg for greater inclusion, equality, reconciliation and communion, these sisters, through their lives and commitments, continue to inspire RSCJ as they journey into the Heart of God.

Epilogue: Seeds Sown

From the 1980s into the early decades of the twenty-first century, some themes central to social justice efforts today were coming into sharper focus, prompting RSCJ to put more energy into certain areas crying out for reform. In particular, RSCJ in the United States Province (later the United States – Canada Province) were moved to action to advocate for peace and development issues related to the imbalance of resources among nations and to address other pressing concerns. These included the continuing effects of racism on Blacks and Native Americans, the need to protect and sustain the earth and its resources, and the problem of uneven access to health care. In this final chapter, we will look at seeds that were planted in each of these areas and briefly celebrate efforts that have begun to bear fruit.

Efforts to Combat Racism

As previous chapters have shown, several RSCJ were deeply engaged in the struggle for Civil Rights during the 1960s and 1970s; and, in efforts to overcome effects of racism, some of the small communities formed by RSCJ to address injustices were inserted among people of color. But it wasn't until the year 2016 that the Religious of the Sacred Heart began to examine the Society's own participation in and benefit from the roots of racism in the United States: the practice of human slavery in the nineteenth century. To begin the research, Provincial Barbara Dawson and her team formed the "Slavery, Accountability and Reconciliation Committee," with a mandate to focus on the Society's role in racism and the enslavement of human beings in the United States.

Through the research undertaken, the committee located descendants of those persons who had been enslaved on the Society's properties in Louisiana, and in 2018, two of the committee members met with them to discuss how the Society might begin to determine means of reparation. One main desire communicated by the descendants was to know where their ancestors were buried and to do something to honor them. In response, an event, entitled "We Say Your Names" was held in September of the same year at the Academy of the Sacred Heart in Grand Coteau, Louisiana, during which Provincial Sheila Hammond, Sister Dawson's successor, acknowledged the Society's complicity in the sin of slavery. At the request of the descendants, the names of their ancestors were inscribed on a monument in the St. Charles Borromeo Jesuit Cemetery, and a plaque with the names of those who had lived there was mounted on the wall of the former slave quarters on the academy grounds.

In the years that followed, descendants and alumnae of color continued to meet with RSCJ to assist the Society with its ongoing anti-racism work. There were regional meetings designed to allow RSCJ to reflect on their own experiences of racism, to understand the systemic nature of racism in the United States, and to learn some helpful vocabulary for future conversations about race. A face-to-face gathering of descendants, persons of color who attended or worked in the Society's schools, RSCJ, and representatives from key groups across the province was held in the fall of 2019 in St. Louis. This meeting was facilitated by Sisters Patricia Chappell and Anne-Louise Nadeau, SNDdeN, who served as anti-racism consultants to the province. Around the same time, a group of Network educators began creating materials for Network schools that would tell the story of the Society's participation in slavery in Louisiana, Missouri, and Kansas, and provide students and teachers with resources for addressing racism. These resources were subsequently posted to the Network's website.

Work with indigenous people

Native Americans have been on the minds of RSCJ in the United States ever since Philippine Duchesne brought the Society to the United States in 1818, along with a deep desire to be a missionary to the Native population. Although Philippine herself would be with Native Americans in Sugar Creek, Kansas, for only one year (1841), the Society's mission of teaching Native American girls in Sugar Creek and St. Marys, Kansas, would continue until 1876. Beyond that, growing awareness of the injustices heaped on Native Americans even into recent times prompted some RSCJ to follow the directives of Philippine's heart by building relationships with Native peoples.

In 1992, Carlota Duarte, RSCJ, realizing that virtually all images of indigenous Mexican Indians had been produced by outsiders, founded the Chiapas Photography Project in Chiapas, Mexico. During Sister Duarte's nearly thirty years of residence in Chiapas, the project empowered indigenous men and women—Mayan Indians—to tell their own stories through photography. With funding support from the Ford Foundation, and mostly donated equipment, the indigenous photographers built an archive of thousands of photographs, many of them also published in books and displayed in galleries. The educational dimensions of the project were twofold, according to Sister Duarte: providing quality education in the art of photography to the Mayan Indians and educating the public about indigenous talent and culture.[128]

About the same time, Marianna Torrano, RSCJ, felt called to live and work on the Soboba Indian Reservation in Southern California. Her ministry included fundraising, spiritual advising, choir directing, and even maintenance and construction work. Over the years, many RSCJ spent time working with Sister Torrano, playing a vital role in restoring the relationship between the Native people and the church. Although many of the Natives had been baptized, they continued to remember a painful past in which they had been abused by representatives of both government and church. Finding that some eight-year-olds could not even write their names, Sister Torrano helped found St. Jude's Mission School on the reservation in 2002 to address the educational needs she witnessed.

In 2014, Sheila Smith, RSCJ, began working closely with a core circle of twelve Ojibwe grandmothers and other groups to fight human trafficking in remote Anishinabek communities in Northern Ottawa. And more recently, Deanna Rose von Bargen, RSCJ, with Molly Arthur, associate, began leading reflection groups to advocate for greater awareness of the injustices suffered by Native Americans, especially in government-sponsored boarding schools operated by religious orders.[129]

Care for Creation

In the early 1980s, persistent, widespread warnings about ongoing degradation to the environment began to inspire creative, grassroots responses from women religious in the Society and other religious orders. Among notable efforts, Miriam MacGillis, OP, started Genesis Farm in New Jersey in 1980 and Paula González, SC, opened La Casa del Sol in Cincinnati in 1985, legendary projects focused on education for ecological sustainability. In the same spirit, in 1982, two RSCJ, Sue Rogers and Margo Morris, both faculty members at Sacred Heart Greenwich (Connecticut), decided to revive a small farm that had previously existed on the school grounds. Eight years later, the farm moved to Poughkeepsie, New York, to a larger farm bequeathed by the estate of Elise Kinkead, so that the project could expand and thrive. They named it Sprout Creek Farm, and Sisters Rogers and Morris, along with a number of other RSCJ who came to help over the next few decades, operated it as a classroom, providing generations of students with opportunities to learn to care for the earth, its resources and its creatures. They did this in part through first-hand experiences with gardening and caring for animals typically found on a farm, such as cows, goats, sheep and chickens. Sadly, Sprout Creek Farm discontinued operations in 2020.[130]

Sister Rogers in 2001 went on to become director of Earthworks, an educational ministry of another religious congregation, the Poor Handmaids of Jesus Christ. Located in northern Indiana, Earthworks was formed to provide and advocate for environmental education and action and to teach children and adults the importance of protecting our fragile natural resources.[131] Among her educational outreach at Earthworks, Sister Rogers directed Project Ready, a baking program designed to teach developmentally disabled adults the connection between food and the environment, while giving them marketable skills.

Eleanor (El) MacLellan, RSCJ, also lent her voice to those warning of a coming ecological crisis. In 1982, she began a twenty-year residency at Drumlin Farm in Lincoln, Massachusetts, where she introduced elementary school students to the complexity and beauty of the natural world. The farm, sponsored by the Massachusetts Audubon Society, gave children a chance to care for farm animals, search pond water for microorganisms, and learn the names of the insects and wild animals in the surrounding forests and fields. Sister MacLellan also traveled to local schools with owls, snakes and other creatures to give inner-city children a chance to experience a bit of nature. She was a tireless advocate for environmentally friendly practices, such as growing organic food, recycling waste, and capturing solar energy.

Mary Patricia Rives, RSCJ, with a special concern for countries with fragile ecosystems, began in the 1980s traveling to the town of San Miguel de Allende in central Mexico every year with groups of students who worked with her and local families to plant trees, build dams and dig ditches to control erosion. She also was an enthusiastic advocate for solar ovens and helped to purchase them for RSCJ communities in Haiti and Africa.[132]

Consciousness about the environmental crisis continues to grow and widen within the province. In the devastating aftermath of Hurricane Katrina in New Orleans in 2005, RSCJ living in Louisiana began to make simple, direct commitments "to address the fragility of God's created world." Those commitments became the bedrock for the "Healthy Waters and Coastal Restoration Interest Group," which, under the leadership of Melanie Guste, RSCJ, has grown to seventy-four members: RSCJ and partners in mission living in six countries, including the United States, Canada, and Mexico. "This ecosystem affects the livelihood of many poor, vulnerable and indigenous persons in our country," said Sister Guste. "In this one place, we can see the devastating effects of massive over-industrialization. A fragmented view of the world is destroying unprecedented amounts of our coastal wetlands, the barrier reefs, and native wildlife."[133]

By the time environmental activist Bill McGibben and others organized the People's Climate March in New York in 2014, several RSCJ were eager to join in, carrying a banner in support of Justice, Peace and Integrity of Creation. Others formulated theological responses. For instance, Mary McGann, RSCJ, has searched for new ways to undergird the movement theologically, exploring, for example, connections between the Eucharist and the way we eat and global food shortages.[134]

Technology at the Service of Social Change

In 1984, Catherine (Kit) Collins, RSCJ, was invited by then-provincial, Nance O'Neil, RSCJ, to create a center where religious and struggling non-profits working for social change in the United States could find help telling their stories as a way to support their missions. In response, Sister Collins opened the Center for Educational Design and Communication (CEDC) in a building the province had acquired in Washington, D.C. Naming their work "Social Justice by Design," the center's staff offered assistance in creating attractive, professionally-done brochures, logos, videos, and eventually webpages that could raise awareness of these organizations' efforts toward systemic change. Over time, the CEDC broadened its focus to include assistance in strategic planning and process facilitation for groups, who often took advantage of the overnight accommodations available at the center. In 2013 the province formed the Stuart Center for Mission at the location to house the CEDC and two recently created offices: the Office of Educational Initiatives and Leadership, and the Office of Justice, Peace and Integrity of Creation (JPIC), among others.

Access to Health Care

Although health has never been a major focus for ministry in the Society, several RSCJ with interests and skills in that area have found ways to offer hope and healing to those on the margins, not only in the United States, but also in other countries, such as Egypt, Africa and Indonesia. In keeping with the Society's expanded sense of education, these new ministries have reflected a broader understanding of the Society's mission to embrace, educate, and heal the whole person. Some RSCJ have operated or worked in clinics or provided mental health services and various kinds of therapy, such as music and art. Others, such as Helen O'Regan, RSCJ, who opened and staffed a clinic for AIDS patients in Kenya, have ministered to people suffering from AIDs.

Mary Margaret (Peggy) McDonnell, RSCJ, began working in Boston's poor neighborhoods in 1973, where she saw firsthand the scarcity of medical resources available to persons living in poverty. What caught her heart, however, was the lack of assistance in the area of medical ethics for sick people facing death and their families. Relying solely on the physicians who treated them, patients had nowhere outside to go to ask for guidance in applying their own value systems to end-of-life questions. Having graduated from Harvard University in 1983 with a master's degree in theology and a concentration in medical ethics, Sister McDonnell had the background to address this gap. Her value-driven work in health care decision-making led in 1995 to the creation of a new non-profit organization called *The Center for Ethics and Advocacy in Healthcare.*[135]

New Forms of International Engagement

A previous chapter in this book on internationality explores in depth the changing understanding of mission after Vatican II and its profound effects on the way RSCJ from the United States Province approached work in other countries and cultures. The Society's commitment to internationality has evolved in recent years, leading to new forms of global engagement. Most notably, the Society internationally heard a call for provinces around the world to begin to work on behalf of the world's poor in a systematic manner. The response was a decision to pursue NGO status at the United Nations so that, as an international congregation of educators with a presence in forty-four countries, the Society might have greater impact at the international level. Cecile Meijer, RSCJ, a member of the United States – Canada Province, was the first director of this NGO office.

From the beginning, the Sacred Heart NGO has worked with the Department of Public Information at the United Nations to disseminate information to the congregation in areas of critical importance, including education, social justice, global interconnectedness and poverty; women, children and youth; migrants and refugees and care for the earth. In 2014, the Society's NGO office was also granted status with the UN's Economic and Social Council. This dual status expanded the Society's role at the UN, making it possible for the Society to not only receive information, but to also engage in advocacy by communicating concerns and experiences from the grassroots to the UN in areas where the Society has special expertise.[136]

On a regional level, the United States – Canada Province has in recent years begun to collaborate with other Society provinces and entities to support regional ministries. For instance, ANAM, consisting of the provincials of Antilles, Mexico, and the United States – Canada provinces, is a new entity formed to support ministries in Haiti; and RSCJ across the provinces of North and South America have come together to create networks such as La Red (for the Society's works of popular education).

In Summary

As this book has shown, the changes in the Society of the Sacred Heart following Vatican II, inspired many sisters to move away from institutional living and to put their faith into concrete action by serving alongside voiceless and vulnerable people living in poverty. For some sisters this service on the periphery took the form of direct service. Others combined direct service with education and advocacy leading to greater self-sufficiency for the people they served. Still others used their gifts as structural thinkers and became actors for systemic and social change. Still others sought systemic change by putting their lives on the line in the peace and civil rights movement. Whatever the way in which they expressed their call to insert themselves into the world, these RSCJ responded to the promptings of the Spirit who led them onto paths, and at times out on limbs, thus far unknown to be available to nuns. Their efforts were powerful contributions to the general movements for change in the larger society. And as this final chapter shows, the Society's members, guided by the Spirit, continue to plant seeds as they seek new, creative ways to bring about the Kingdom of God on earth.

Endnotes

[1] https://www.vatican.va/archive/hist_councils/ii_vatican_council/documents/vat-ii_decree_19651028_perfectae-caritatis_en.html

[2] Marie Augusta Neal, SNDdeN (Mystic Connecticut: Twenty-Third Publications, 1990.)

[3] Lora Ann Quiñonez, CDP, and Mary Daniel Turner, SNDdeN (Philadelphia: Temple University Press, 1993).

[4] This is true especially after my service with the Leadership Conference of Women Religious ten years ago. See *Spiritual Leadership in Challenging Times* (Maryknoll, NY: Orbis Books, 2013).

[5] (New York: The New American Library, 1968).

[6] *Lettres circulaires,* January 10, 1964, 129-138. Quoted in Monique Luirard, RSCJ, *The Society of the Sacred Heart in the World of Its Times: 1865-2000,* trans., Frances Gimber (Society of the Sacred Heart, St. Louis, Mo., 2016), 475.

[7] This is not a comprehensive overview of Vatican II. There is much literature available for those who wish to study this important period more deeply.

[8] While many have *responded* positively to the initiatives of Vatican II, this is not true universally. Over the past fifty-five years there have been resistances as well as responses.

[9] Second Vatican Council, "Pastoral Constitution on the Church in the Modern World." *Gaudium et spes* 1965, par.1. http://www.vatican.va/archive/hist_councils/ii_vatican_council/documents/vat-ii_const_19651207_gaudium-et-spes_en.html

[10] Ibid., par. 3 and 4.

[11] Second Vatican Council, "Dogmatic Constitution on the Church," *Lumen Gentium.* Chapter II uses this extensively. https://www.vatican.va/archive/hist_councils/ii_vatican_council/documents/vat-ii_const_19641121_lumen-gentium_en.html

[12] Ibid. par. 40

[13] It should be noted that the process of change exacted a significant cost to the Society, its members and Sabine de Valon herself.

[14] Only eighteen years after its foundation, the Society of the Sacred Heart sent missionaries in the persons of Philippine Duchesne and four companions to the Louisiana Purchase territory. Philippine's ambition was to evangelize Native Americans; she was sent to work with them only at the end of her life. Before that she opened schools for children of European and American settlers.

[15] Luirard, *Society*, 463.

[16] The title alluded to the words of Philippine Duchesne when she begged to be sent to mission in America.

[17] *Mitte me,* N° 1, Introduction of Françoise de Lambilly, 1.

[18] Luirard, *Society,* 464.

[19] Ibid. 43. 1% served in Latin America, 33.3% in Africa and 24.48% in Asia. See note 30.

[20] General Archives, Society of the Sacred Heart, D I 3 e Box 1 (Hereafter Arch. Gén.). They taught, organized youth movements, occupied themselves with social work, worked in dispensaries, and visited families of prisoners and rag pickers in Monterrey. Latin Americans were trained on the spot to work in their own country.

[21] *Mitte me,* 1962, No. 3, 24. Quoted in Luirard, 466.

[22] The foundation was made by an Irish nun, Mother Ivy Bourke, three Indian, an English and a Maltese religious.

[23] *Mitte me,* 1962, No. 3, 23. Quoted in Luirard, 466.

[24] "The alumnae had contributed in 1958 to the creation in this section of a parish under the title of Saint Madeleine Sophie; the school founded in 1963 was named *Madre admirable*." In Colombia, certain ones among them made use of a diocesan radio relay station that evangelized the local populations.

[25] Ibid.

[26] Constitutions of the Society of the Sacred Heart, 1815. #5. V.

[27] Luirard, *Society*, 474.

[28] The Society is officially named an apostolic *institute* of pontifical right, but the term congregation is usually better understood in referring to religious life.

[29] Luirard, *Society,* 529.

[30] Special Chapter 1967, Orientations *ad experimentum*, 20-21. (U.S. version).

[31] Society of the Sacred Heart of Jesus, *Directives and Decisions of the 26th General Congregation,* 26-27 and 33.

[32] In 1965 the number was increased to include ten religious, two major superiors of Oriental Rite having been introduced, and thirteen laywomen.

[33] Luirard, Society, 476.

[34] Frances M. Gimber, RSCJ, *Woman of the Word*: A Life of Marie Louise Schroen, RSCJ: 1909-1991 (St. Louis, Mo.: Society of the Sacred Heart, United States Province, 1991), 148-149.

[35] Choir and coadjutrix sisters had different prayer schedules, opportunities for conversation and education, among other differences. They also wore different crosses and rings. It was essentially a two-class system, even as the vocation to the Society was the same.

[36] Luirard, 476.

[37] Ibid. 486-487.

[38] Ibid., 530.

[39] *Orientations*, 19, 25.

[40] *Orientations*, 37. See Luirard, *Society*, 530-531.

[41] Luiard, *Society*, 531.

[42] *Orientations*, 41.

[43] Testimony of Francisca Tamayo. While the vicars accepted sending their novices to Frascati, they asked to have them back after their first vows. See Luirard, *Society*, 463.

[44] Arch. Gén. C I C 3, Box 21. Report of Congo. Mother Keogh gave the same advice: to be a missionary one must be astonished at nothing. Found in Luirard, *Society*, 533.

[45] Arch. Gén. C I C 3. Report of Congo. See Luirard, 533-534.

[46] Synod of Bishops, Justice in the World, 1971. See https://www.cctwincities.org/wp-content/uploads/2015/10/Justicia-in-Mundo.pdf

[47] Now called "professed of temporary vows."

[48] (Lanham, Maryland: Rowman and Littlefield, 2003).

[49] (Lanham, Maryland: University Press of America, 1985).

[50] (New York: Paulist Press, 1986).

[51] Madeleine Sophie Barat, now Saint Madeleine Sophie, was canonized by Pope Pius XI in May 24, 1925.

[52] Preparation for perpetual profession.

[53] Copyright Ephpheta House, Farmington, Michigan, 1974. Available in LP vinyl at discocom.

[54] Special Chapter 1967, Orientation ad experimentum, 64 (US version)

[55] The code is available online at https://www.vatican.va/archive/cod-iuris-canonici/cic_index_en.html

[56] "Dynamic equivalence" in language translation strives to render in modern language the intent, meaning, and spirit of the original text rather than adhere rigidly to the form and structure of the original.

[57] Avery Dulles, Dulles, Avery. *Models of the Church* expanded edition (Garden City N.Y: Image Books, 1978).

[58] Archives Society of the Sacred Heart, United States – Canada Province, Katharine Hargrove obituary.

[59] Ibid.

[60] (D. and F. Scott Publishing, 1998)

[61] Archives, unpublished manuscript.

[62] Archives, excerpt from Sister Fiske's diary, typescript.

[63] Archives, Elizabeth Hoye, obituary.

[64] Alison Van Dyk: https://templeofunderstanding.org/wp-content/uploads/2018/10/sr.-kirby-un-memorial.pdf

[65] Joan Kirby, obituary, https://rscj.org/about/memoriam/joan-kirby-rscj

[66] The United Nations' eight "Millenium Development Goals," formulated in 2000, commit world leaders to combat poverty and disease and to promote education, health, gender equality, and environmental sustainability.

[67] (St. Louis, Mo.: Society of the Sacred Heart, United States – Canada Province, 2016.)

[68] Paulo Freire, *Pedagogy of the Oppressed: 30th Anniversary Edition*, 1970 translation of the 1968 Portuguese original (Bloomsbury, 2014), 54.

[69] (CreateSpace Amazon, 2016). CreateSpace was replaced in 2018 by Kindle Direct Publishing. (KDP).

[70] Journal of Baha'í Studies, vol. 25, no. 3 (2015)

[71] *Les temps changent, et il faut aussi modifier et changer.* Letter to Philippine Duchesne, November 30, 1831.

[72] John Goodlad (1920-1914) was an educational researcher noted for developing models for renewing schools and educating teachers.

[73] John I. Goodlad, *Education News*, September 1968.

[74] Patricia Barrett, "My Ministry with the Poor," Archives. USC Province, St. Louis, Missouri.

[75] Rosemary Dowd, RSCJ, "Preaching Love and Forgiveness Where There is No Love," *Heart* magazine, Society of the Sacred Heart, Winter 2013, 18-19. https://rscj.org/system/files/publications/attachments/heart_winter_2013_0.pdf

[76] *A Precious Fountain: Music in the Worship of an African-American Catholic Community* (Collegeville, MN: Liturgical Press, 2004).

[77] The following RSCJ served at the Thensted Center: Joan Ewing, Nancy Bremner, Mike Hoffman, Marie-Louise Wolfington, Georgeann Parisek. In addition, Anne Byrne, Therese Downey, Betty Renard, Mary Kay Hunyady, and Bonnie Kearney, all RSCJ, spent time at both the Academy of the Sacred Heart in Grand Coteau and at the Thensted Center. Alice Mills, RSCJ, offered counseling services.

[78] "Little Sisters, Big-Time Services in East Harlem," *Heart* magazine, Society of the Sacred Heart, Summer 2007, 11-14. https://rscj.org/system/files/publications/attachments/heart---summer-2007_0.pdf.

[79] Second Vatican Council, "Pastoral Constitution on The Church in The Modern World," *Gaudium et Spes, https://www.vatican.va/archive/hist_councils/ii_vatican_council/documents/vat-ii_const_19651207_gaudium-et-spes_en.html.*

[80] Peter Henriot, "Remembering 'Justice': Retrieving a Forgotten Proclamation," *America,* November 14, 2011. https://www.americamagazine.org/issue/794/article/remembering-justice.

[81] Rosa Carbonell, *María Josefa Bultó Blajot, RSCJ, 1905-2011* (Sociedad del Sagrado Corazón), 148).

[82] Exclaustration was a formal permission granted to a vowed religious allowing her to live outside of community for a period of time.

[83] Other RSCJ who lived in or volunteered at Sursum Corda over the years included Julie Yachtis, Joan Ewing, Deanna Rose Von Bargen, Helen McCulloch, Margaret Mary Coakley, and Marilyn Lorenz.

[84] Shell Trap, a Saul Alinsky-trained organizer from Chicago, came to Sursum Corda and ran a workshop for all the tenant associations in the neighborhood.

[85] The name of the university was changed to University of Notre Dame de Namur in 2001.

[86] Society of the Sacred Heart, United States Province, "An Act of Hope: Province Priorities for Strategic Planning," United States Province, 1992. https://stuartcenter.org/updates/administration-an-act-of-hope

[87] Second Vatican Council, "Pastoral Constitution on the Church in the Modern World." *Gaudium et spes* 1965, par.1. http://www.vatican.va/archive/hist_councils/ii_vatican_council/documents/vat-ii_const_19651207_gaudium-et-spes_en.html

[88] For more about the community in Nicaragua see the autobiography of Mary Catherine McKay on the *JPIC Ministries after Vatican II* website: https://jpicbook.stuartcenter.org/ministries?name=mckay

[89] Wangari Maathai, Nobel Lecture, Oslo, Norway (December 10, 2004). Available at https://www.nobelprize.org/prizes/peace/2004/maathai/lecture/, visited August 10, 2020.

[90] In this context, it is important to remember that between 1967 and 1982, the Society of the Sacred Heart in the United States was still organized in five different provinces: San Francisco, Chicago, Boston, New York, and St. Louis. The U.S. Province as such was born only in 1982.

[91] International Education Commission Working Paper, *Education: A Commitment*, 1988, page 13.

[92] Sister McDonnell's role in *Sursum Corda* is described in another chapter of this book, "Community Organizing." In this chapter, her efforts on behalf of housing rights are presented in abbreviated form as a necessary steppingstone to understanding how RSCJ began to grasp their role as agents of change.

[93] From Sister McDonnell's obituary. This obituary and all others referenced are found in the Archives of the USC Province. They may be obtained upon request to archives@rscj.org.

[94] *The Washington Post* of July 4, 2004, *Sister Katherine McDonnell*, available at https://www.washingtonpost.com/archive/local/2004/07/04/sister-katherine-mcdonnell/b42e0657-2ec5-4574-9e12-22edd24d4f6f/, accessed September 27, 2020.

[95] From Sister McDonnell's obituary.

[96] Ibid.

[97] Serving on boards of directors of various social service agencies in Washington, D.C., was one more way for Sister McDonnell to stand up and defend the rights of those living in poverty.

[98] See Sister Joan Kirby's obituary, https://rscj.org/about/memoriam/joan-kirby-rscj, accessed September 4, 2021.

[99] Patricia Burns, *The Shamrock and the Shield: An Oral History of the Irish in Montreal* (Montreal: Vehicule Press, 1998), 77. In this book, Sister Power tells her own story.

[100] See, for example, Paulo Freire, *Pedagogy of the Oppressed*, Fiftieth Anniversary Edition, trans. Myra Bergman Ramos (New York: Bloomsbury Academic, 2000).

[101] Burns, *The Shamrock and the Shield*, 77.

[102] Ibid., 78.

[103] Ibid.

[104] Much of the following information was taken from a recording of Sister Mardel's story, *Mary Mardel in Her Own Words: Behind Bars with the Farmworkers*; see *JPIC Ministries after Vatican II* webpage.

[105] This was most likely Sister Trudy Patch, provincial team member during Sister Mardel's tenure as provincial.

[106] See Mary Mardel, available in *JPIC Ministries after Vatican II* webpage https://jpicbook.stuartcenter.org/ministry/mary-be-mardel.

[107] Letter for the Feast of the Sacred Heart 2020, by Superior General Sister Barbara Dawson, dated June, 19, 2020, available at https://RSCJinternational.org/news/feast-sacred-heart-2020, accessed September 12, 2020.

[108] See *JPIC Ministries Online Archive*: https://jpicbook.stuartcenter.org/.

[109] Telephone conversation with Sister Tobin in August 2020. The Pastoral Letter to the People of God in El Paso by Bishop Mark Joseph Seitz, written following the Walmart massacre on August 3, 2019, develops what Sister Tobin mentions. In this letter, Bishop Seitz reflects on racism, institutionalized racism and white supremacy in the context of life in the Texas borderlands. *See* Mark Joseph Seitz, Bishop of El Paso, *Night will be no more*, October 13, 2019, available at https://www.hopeborder.org/nightwillbenomore-eng, accessed August 31, 2020.

[110] Quoted in *JPIC Ministries Online Archive*: https://jpicbook.stuartcenter.org/

[111] Telephone conversation between the author and Sister Lasseigne in September 2020.

[112] Ibid.

[113] "The Cubans leaving Cuba from the port of Mariel to come to the United States between April 15 and October 31, 1980. Fidel Castro had decided to 'let' them leave—many were simply taken out of jails and mental hospitals and put on boats. Approximately 125,000 Cubans arrived in Florida." Quoted from "A refugee would love to have your problems," in *JPIC Ministries Online Archive:* jpicbook.StuartCenter.org

[114] The government agency known as the Immigration and Naturalization Service (INS) stopped operating as an entity in 2003. Most of its functions were transferred to the umbrella of the newly created Department of Homeland Security and were divided among the following agencies: U.S. Immigration Services. U.S. Immigration and Customs Enforcement, and U.S. Customs and Border Protection Services.

[115] See *JPIC Ministries Online Archive:* https://jpicbook.stuartcenter.org/

[116] *The Gong*, April 5, 1965. See *JPIC Ministries Online Archive:* jpicbook.StuartCenter.org

[117] Patricia Barrett RSCJ, *Ministry with the Poor*, dated 1984-85, in *JPIC Ministries Online Archive:* https://jpicbook.stuartcenter.org/.

[118] Martha Curry, RSCJ, *Barat College: a Legacy, a Spirit, and a Name* (Chicago: Loyola Press, 2012), 141-2.

[119] Following a Plowshares action in 1985, Sister Montgomery was named as a defendant in a lawsuit filed in federal district court, "United Sates v. Sister Anne Montgomery et al."

[120] Blessing by Superior General Kathleen Conan, RSCJ, and Provincial Paula Toner, March 27, 2011. Society of the Sacred Heart Archives, XII. C. Montgomery.

[121] From Sister Coakley's obituary.

[122] See *JPIC Ministries Online Archive:* https://jpicbook.stuartcenter.org/.

[123] Unless otherwise indicated, this section is largely based on information provided by email and phone by Sisters Anne O'Neil and Marina Hernandez in September and October 2020.

[124] The stewardship committee had the following members: Sisters Bonnie Kearney, Mary Bernstein, Maggie Fisher, Maureen Kelly, Margaret Munch, and Dean Traynor.

[125] MCRI later became a member of the Interfaith Center on Corporate Responsibility (ICCR).

[126] The "rand" is the official currency of South Africa since the country's independence in 1961. Paul Kruger was a South African statesman in the late nineteenth century, who is remembered as the builder of the Afrikaner nation. *See* https://www.britannica.com/biography/Paul-Kruger.

Although importing the Krugerrand was illegal in many western countries, the United States banned its import only in 1985. The import ban was lifted in later years. *See* https://en.wikipedia.org/wiki/Krugerrand. Both websites in this footnote were accessed August 18, 2020.

[127] See *JPIC Ministries Online Archive: http://*jpicbook.StuartCenter.org

[128] Society of the Sacred Heart, Heart magazine, Winter 2006, 11-14. https://rscj.org/publications/heart-magazine-winter-2006-vol-4-no-3

[129] See Maureen's Chicoine's book, *Grave on the Prairie*, for more information about the Sacred Heart school for children of the Citizen Potawatomi Nation in Kansas from 1841 until 1879.

[130] For more information on the farm's closing, see https://rscj.org/news/sprout-creek-farm-transfers-control-operations-marist-college

[131] See *Heart* magazine, Spring 2012, 2007. https://rscj.org/system/files/publications/attachments/heart_spring_2012_for_website.pdf

[132] "South of the Border, Hearts Expand," Heart magazine, Spring 2007, 11-14 https://rscj.org/news/publications/category/heart-magazine/

[133] See Heart magazine, Spring 2012, 13-14. https://rscj.org/news/publications/category/heart-magazine

[134] Mary E. McGann, RSCJ, *The Meal That Reconnects: Eucharistic Eating and the Global Food Crisis* (Collegeville MN: Liturgical Press, 2020)

[135] For more information, see M. Margaret McDonnell, RSCJ, *The Golden Thread: Making Healthcare Decisions in Neighborhoods* (Balboa Press, self-publishing division of Hay House Publishing, 2022).

[136] See Society of the Sacred Heart at the UN: https://rscj.org/society-sacred-heart-united-nations.

Our Contributors

Many people helped bring this book to fruition. In 2015, the provincial team of the United States – Canada Province of the Society of the Sacred Heart realized that the stories of the women who had been pioneers of so many social justice initiatives in the 1960s and 1970s were in danger of being lost unless an effort was made to preserve them. In response to this concern, the USC Province Publications Committee worked with Diane Roche, RSCJ, and Bonnie Kearney, RSCJ, and a team of researchers and writers who gathered the stories and grouped them thematically.

Below are brief biographies of the authors of the chapters of this book.

Maria Cimperman, RSCJ, is Associate Professor of Theological Ethics at Catholic Theological Union, Chicago, and founding director of the Center for the Study of Consecrated Life at CTU. Her interests include engaging contemporary expressions of consecrated life and exploring the ways global calls are lived in particular contexts. Most recently, she is the author of *Religious Life For Our World: Creating Communities of Hope* and co-editor of *Engaging Our Diversity: Interculturality and Consecrated Life Today*, both published by Orbis Books in 2020. With a desire to build an international resource community, she is currently a member of a team organizing a gathering of women religious theologians from around the world. She authored the chapter "Vatican II and the Society of the Sacred Heart."

Frances Gimber, RSCJ, met the Society as a student at what is now Sacred Heart Schools, Atherton, California. After graduating from Manhattanville College of the Sacred Heart, she entered the Society and spent several years as a teacher and administrator in Sacred Heart schools in the East; she was then sent to the International School in Tokyo in 1988 to teach English and religion. When she returned three years later, she worked briefly at Newton Country Day School of the Sacred Heart before being called to the motherhouse in Rome to be secretary to the superior general. She returned to the United States in 2001 and shortly afterwards was asked to take over the direction of the archives of the Society's United States Province in St. Louis. She retired after seven years and at present serves the province as an editor and proofreader. She was co-editor of this book, for which she wrote "The Way We Were: Life Before Vatican II."

Kathleen Hughes, RSCJ, entered the Society of the Sacred Heart in 1962 after graduating from Newton College of the Sacred Heart. She was the first woman to receive a doctorate in Liturgical Studies from the University of Notre Dame in 1981, served as Professor of Word and Worship at the Catholic Theological Union in Chicago from 1980 to 1999, and served one term as academic dean. In 1999, she became provincial of the Society's United States Province. Following a post-provincial sabbatical, she has been contributing to the province's formation to mission efforts in schools and communities across the country. Sister Hughes was a member of the advisory board of the International Commission on English in the Liturgy (ICEL) for two decades and chaired the subcommittee that prepared original texts for worship among English speakers across the world. She has written or edited eleven books and has published numerous articles and reviews demonstrating a broad range of interest in worship, sacraments, preaching, language, feminism, and spirituality. She authored the chapter "New Roles for Women After Vatican II."

Bonnie Kearney, RSCJ, attended Convent of the Sacred Heart in Lake Forest, Illinois, then Manhattanville College and Barat College. Early in her teaching ministry, she worked in Sacred Heart schools in Chicago, Ohio, and Nebraska, and in the late 1970s felt called to work with students in schools on the margins. She taught in a technical school and in several all-Black high schools, some in Cabrini Green in Chicago and in inner city Houston. She worked twice in Indonesia and began a program for children in the Catholic Charities family shelter system in Chicago. Most recently she administered Duchesne House for Volunteers in New Orleans. She authored three chapters: "Ecumenical and Interfaith Ventures," "Educational Projects for the Underserved," and "New Initiatives in Sacred Heart Schools."

Cecile Meijer, RSCJ, grew up in The Netherlands and has lived in the United States since the mid-1980s. Since earning an LL.M. degree in the protection of human rights within the context of international law in 1993, she has been an advocate for groups of marginalized persons. Through long experience at the United Nations in New York as the NGO representative of the international Society of the Sacred Heart, she has learned how to transpose her legal background into effective inter-congregational advocacy for social change and equity on a global scale—in short, advocating for systemic change. She has a special interest in justice, peace, and integrity of creation, especially in issues related to social protection, equality, equity, interculturality, and international politics. She authored the chapter "Working for Systemic Change and Human Rights."

Lolin Menéndez, RSCJ, was born to Spanish parents who went to Puerto Rico in the aftermath of civil war. Her education began in the Sacred Heart school in the capital, and she went on to study in Madrid; Newton, Massachusetts; Purchase, New York; and Paris before entering the novitiate at Kenwood in Albany, New York. After teaching in Sacred Heart schools in Bethesda, Maryland, and Miami, she heeded the call to Africa, where she ministered for twenty-seven years, forming teachers and parish leaders and coordinating education programs for Jesuit Refugee Service. She served as webweaver of rscjinternational.org for its first five years, working from Rome, and now serves in Puerto Rico as provincial secretary and archivist. The dimensions of internationality and the involvement in the world of peoples on the move remain at the heart of her ministry. She authored the chapter titled "Internationality."

Mary Novak began serving as executive director of NETWORK Lobby for Catholic Social Justice in April 2021 and is the first lay person to lead the organization. She is a lawyer, educator, chaplain, spiritual director, and activist who has worked in Catholic contexts for decades. Before leading NETWORK, she served as associate director of mission integraton and as a law professor at Georgetown University. She chairs the advisory board of the Initiative on Restorative Justice and Healing at the University of St. Thomas Law School. She agreed to write the foreword to this book soon after the gala celebrating the fiftieth anniversary of the founding of NETWORK, during which three RSCJ were honored as being among the "founding mothers."

Diane Roche, RSCJ, has spent the better part of four decades living and working in poor, urban neighborhoods in the United States and Haiti. Her training and deepest interest is in the field of affordable housing. She has been a property manager in Boston, St. Louis, and Washington, D.C., and executive director for several nonprofit community development agencies. She served the Society of the Sacred Heart as director of ministry for the United States Province, JPIC director for the United States – Canada Province, and member of the provincial team, as well as a trustee of several Sacred Heart schools. She earned a bachelor's degree in English from Emmanuel College in Boston and a master's in urban affairs from Boston University. Diane wrote three chapters: "Works of Mercy," "Community Organizing," and "Epilogue: Seeds Sown."

Suzanne Rogers, RSCJ, after a number of years as a teacher and administrator in Sacred Heart Network schools, spent twenty-five years teaching environmental and spiritual values to children and adults at working farms in New York and Indiana. She initiated and for several summers led a summer program called the American Experience, an educational tour of the United States for high school girls. She is currently working as innkeeper and team member at EncounterPoint in Chicago, a welcoming and sacred space for groups and individuals to encounter self, others, and the Spirit of God. She contributed to the section on the environment in "Epilogue: Seeds Sown."

Acknowledgements

From the moment in 2015 when Barbara Dawson, provincial, and her provincial team expressed the desire for this book, it was clear that many voices would be needed in order to tell multiple aspects of the story. Those who wrote the various chapters are acknowledged in brief biographies above. There are, however, many others without whose assistance this book could never have come into being.

Frances Gimber, RSCJ, as chairperson of the USC Province Publications Committee, accepted the task of finding a person to shepherd the project. Diane Roche, RSCJ, and later Bonnie Kearney, RSCJ, took responsibility for identifying themes and authors for each chapter and coordinating their work. A small group of consultants, including RSCJ Martha Curry and Carlota Duarte, gave much valuable advice on how to proceed. The RSCJ on the committee, Mary Charlotte Chandler, Kathleen Hughes, Juliet Mousseau and Carolyn Osiek, spent many hours working with Sisters Roche and Kearney to keep the project moving forward through the many stages of research and identifying themes and authors.

The authors' work would not have been possible without the painstaking research of Michael Pera, assistant archivist. With support from Carolyn Osiek, RSCJ, at the Archives of the Society of the Sacred Heart, he located, scanned and emailed hundreds of documents and photos to supply material to those who were writing the chapters and to help create the on-line profiles of justice-minded RSCJ from the past and present. These profiles can be found in the online JPIC archive that is the companion to this book.

Linda Kato, RSCJ, spent hours searching through and organizing the avalanche of emailed responses from members of the province to a request for stories and names of people that should be part of the book and the online archive. She also did research using public sources to corroborate and add depth to many of these stories. Her research and analytical skills made it possible to handle the volume of material sent from around the Society.

Pamela Schaeffer, an associate of the Society of the Sacred Heart and founding editor of *Heart* Magazine, accepted the task of shepherding the project once the authors had submitted their work, bringing her forty years of editorial experience to the arduous task of editing the complicated manuscript. She was assisted in this by Sister Gimber. For decisions regarding style, the editors relied on The Chicago Manual of Style, sixteenth edition; the online Liturgical Press Style Guide, and an internal style guide created especially for editing publications of the United States – Canada Province.

Carole Sargent, also an associate of the Society, and director of the Office of Scholarly Publications at Georgetown University, as well as a published author, provided advice at key points during the process, supplied the software and helped to create the index.

Laryn Kragt-Bakker formerly of the Center for Educational Design and Communication patiently created a series of online tools to help gather, organize and present the stories that surfaced from across the province to form the online JPIC Archive.

Beth Ponticello, creative director of the Center for Educational Design and Communication, designed the book. She created the cover, designed the display of photographs in the center of the book, and laid out the text.

We extend our warmest thanks to each of these people and to all who through their interest, their contributions and encouragement helped to make the book possible.

Index

C

D

E

F

G

H

I

M

N

O

P

Q

R

S

T

U

V

Printed in the USA
CPSIA information can be obtained
at www.ICGtesting.com
LVHW071050270923
PP17902600006B/22